Search For Understanding

**Lutheran Conversations
with Reformed,
Anglican, and
Roman Catholic
Churches**

WARREN A. QUANBECK

AUGSBURG PUBLISHING HOUSE
MINNEAPOLIS, MINNESOTA

SEARCH FOR UNDERSTANDING

Copyright © 1972 Augsburg Publishing House

Library of Congress Catalog Card No. 72-90259

International Standard Book No. 0-8066-1306-8

Manufactured in the United States of America

CONTENTS

6

FOREWORD

The twentieth century will be known in future church history books as the beginning of the great effort to bring the Christian churches together again — as the search for understanding.

Christians have always believed that they were one people. It is part of their basic confession of faith: "I believe . . . in the holy Christian church." But never in history have they been able to fully manifest that oneness God has given to them.

After several centuries of new divisions and schisms, Christians in our time have begun to work together, locally, nationally, and even internationally, in caring for the needs of the world. Councils of churches have been formed to assist in communication, study, and common work. This followed the New Testament example of the Council at Jerusalem which brought together Christians who were having a dispute in the time of Peter and Paul. World Conferences have been held to study the faith and attempt to reconcile differences, and to plan strategy in mission. Living room dialogues have helped lay people to discuss their faith with their neighbors.

In the last decade, the search for understanding carried on by direct confrontation and conversation between churches, two at a time, has been very fruitful. These are known as bi-lateral conversations. This book aims to tell you about the three important ones which have engaged the Lutherans on both a national and an international level.

You may have many questions about these conversations. How could new understanding come about? Were our forefathers wrong? Have we compromised the faith? What has happened to bring about these new situations?

I hope this book will help you to answer these questions. These matters should not be confined to theologians at small meetings but exposed to the whole church for study and reaction. When everyone has had an opportunity to read and understand, the search for understanding will have made a giant step forward.

KENT S. KNUTSON

THE CHURCH
AND THE
UNITY OF
MANKIND

There is today widespread disappointment with the Christian church. Practicing Christians discover that the institutional church offers them less than they want from it. Less ardent members seem to get very little from their association with the church. They are not opposed to it; they just ignore it. Among earnest young people the institutional church is high on the list for remodeling, drastic alteration or abolition. Why is this?

Most people who are well informed about the church would agree that the problem is not wide-spread corruption or immorality. The leaders of the church are men of earnestness and good character. Most church members are decent people and respected by their neighbors. Church organizations are administered with fair efficiency and devote a substantial share of their total income and energy to works that are at least intended to help people. Yet the very virtues of the church seem badly tarnished. The decency of its members seems a drab self-righteousness. The life of the congregations appears to be dull and tedious. The leaders seem earnest but commonplace, dedicated but routine, faithful but unimaginative. The church's worship seems like the turning of a prayer wheel, and its program of service lamentably inadequate to the needs of the day.

Question has even arisen about its mission. Doubts are expressed not only about the missionary effectiveness of the church, but about the very idea of a world mission of the church.

Yet in the midst of all that is drab and commonplace in the church, there are signs of life and hope. There is faithfulness, there are works of love, there are living congregations, and there is a vision of what the church should be. Especially among young people this vision fires zeal for a church which is really the church. People continue to offer their lives to God. Their eagerness, their generosity, sometimes even their impatience, are like the coming of rain to the parched ground.

Many factors contribute to the growth of the yearning for renewal: the deeply felt awareness of critical problems in the life of the nation; the painful contrast between the affluence of America and the terrible poverty of the third world; frustration at the inadequate results of evangelistic and missionary programs; the encounter with Christians of other traditions and a resultant impatience with all that separates us from them in worship and service; the recovery of the biblical image of the church as God's people in the world; not simply a rescue mission for lost souls, but God's instrument for the redemption and restoration of his creation. There is a stirring in almost all church bodies, and in some of them such widespread challenge to traditional patterns of theology and church life that a revolution seems to be under way.

The Rediscovery of the Church

The recovery of the biblical vision of the church reminds us that many of our ways of speaking of the church are strange to the Scriptures. We speak of the church as building, as denomination, (the Lutheran church), as synod, (the Lutheran Church in America), the church convention or the machinery of church headquarters ("the church has decided something or other"), or in the jargon of the sociologist, one of the factors in the life of modern society. None of these usages would be familiar to a member of the early church, and all of them would seem improper and misleading. The early Christians could accept only two of our common uses of the word "church": the local congregation, the people of God gathered in this place, and the church universal, the people of God throughout the world. The New Testament does not distinguish between them. There is only one people of God, for God is one. God's people are dispersed throughout the world. At the same time the people of God in this place is fully the people of God, a living organism which serves God in worship, witness and in service to the world.

The writers of the New Testament project their understanding of the church and its mission in a variety of pictures, most of them taken from the religious vocabulary of the old Israel, but some borrowed from their contemporary world. They do not use abstract terms to describe it, but invite us to a picture gallery where many different images attract us, stimulate our imaginations, and stir us to awareness of what a wonderful thing God has done in calling a people to his service in the world.

They call it "people of God"; this is what the term "church" means, the people called by God to serve him in the world and to make him known to all nations. The people of God have a calling, a mission, a purpose in the world; a calling to be God's servants or instruments to restore his rule in the world and to make it once again what God created it to be.

They call it the temple of God. It is the community in which God is present, where he does his gracious work, and where he can be known, worshipped and served. Temple in the Old Testament referred to a building. The term "temple" applied to the church refers to a community of people whose most remarkable quality is that God is among them in his love and power. If men want to know where God is, the answer of the New Testament is clear —in the community of Christians.

They call the church God's field or God's vine. By this they indicate that God has a purpose for his church. He plants and cultivates his field or vineyard and expects to harvest a crop. The picture of the vine emphasizes this purpose very clearly (Ezek. 15, John 15); a vine produces no lumber, poor firewood, and not even a decent pot-hook. If it bears no fruit it is a completely useless thing.

Paul calls the church the body of Christ, suggesting that the Christian community is the bodily presence in the world of the risen and regnant Christ. Jesus Christ gave himself for the life of the world, healing the sick, cleansing lepers, restoring sight and hearing to the blind and deaf, and preaching good news to the poor. The church as the body of Christ is also called to show the love of God in a variety of ways: proclaiming good news, being a healing community, reaching out to the rejected and lost, and giving its life for the life of the world.

The church is therefore not merely an insurance society formed to protect its members from the more unpleasant aspects of the hereafter. It is the agency, the community through which God does his saving work in the present, reconciling men to himself and to each other, restoring their integrity as persons and giving proper relationships to other persons, to society and to the entire creation. Theologians used to speak of the church as the "supernatural community." By this they meant that God is present and active in the church. For this reason the church channels the blessings of God to men and restores to life in the world the dimension it needs to be genuine and real. The entire creation was made to live in harmony with its Creator. Sin is the destruction of that harmony, redemption is its restoration. What the church offers in the gospel is nothing less than the restoration of true humanity, human life lived in its proper relationship to God and to the rest of the creation.

One, Holy, Catholic, Apostolic

This recovery of the biblical understanding of the church frees us from our depression about the powerlessness, conventionality and triviality of much that we have labelled "church." It enables us to acknowledge our faults and those of our church bodies and also liberates us to seek to become the real and living church as God wills that we should. It also helps us to understand some of the ways in which Christians have spoken of the church in the past. When, for example, men spoke of the church as one, holy, catholic and apostolic we can see these words, not as abstractions, but as words which describe the living reality of the church as God's people on earth, and to see how they help us understand what we ought to be as a Christian community.

To say that the church is apostolic is to say that it has a living and genuine connection with the church founded by Jesus Christ. The church lives by the proclamation of the apostolic message, is vivified by the continuing acts of God in the sacraments, and carries out its mission of worship, witness and service in the world. It is a church sent by Christ, living by his continually renewed presence in its midst, and responsible to him for all its life and work.

The term catholic has become for many connected with the Roman Catholic church and has therefore come to mean a quality of exclusiveness. Its original meaning is precisely the opposite. Catholic means universal, or ecumenical. It emphasizes that as the people of God the church is above all human differences of race, color, nation, economic class, or social status. The church of Christ exists for all people, is open to all, and seeks to bring all into obedience to their proper Lord.

To speak of the church as holy can also cause misunderstanding. For holiness means to many today the prim virtue of a plaster saint, or the self-conscious rectitude of the Pharisee. To ascribe such holiness to the church does not make it attractive, but to many rather repellent—a sanctimonious society which ought at all costs to be avoided. But holiness, according to the New Testament, means to be set aside for the use and service of God. Quite ordinary or even unworthy people can become holy by being joined to the mission of Christ. The church is such a fellowship of ordinary humans and is given its exceptional character by being set aside to the service of God, and by his presence in its midst. The holiness of the church is thus never the holiness of human achievement, but rather the holiness of Christ himself.

The unity of the church is also its unity in Christ. It is not a unity engineered by church officials or theologians, but the unity given by God in the gift of his Son. There is only one Christ, one gospel, one church. All who belong to Christ through baptism and faith are members of this one church. In spite of the divisions in Christendom there is only one church of God, which exists wherever Christ does his saving work through the gospel.

Unity for the Sake of Mission

People will ask: if there is a unity of the church in Jesus Christ which exists in spite of all divisions, is not this spiritual unity sufficient? God knows who belongs to him and therefore the divisions in the church are no more serious than the existence of competing chains of grocery stores. The competition may even be healthy for the denominations!

It is true that where evangelical motivations are lacking and Christians do not feel themselves constrained by the love of Christ, a healthy kind of competition may provide motive power. When men are not drawn to God by the gospel they may be driven to him by the law. But Christian unity cannot be a purely spiritual thing, visible only to God. Nor can it be an entirely future matter, to be disclosed only on the day of judgment. The unity of the people of God in Christ should become visible in the life of God's people, in their worship, witness, service, and structure. If it does not become visible one important dimension of the reality of the church is missing. For as the Father sent his Son to reconcile his creatures to himself, so the Son has sent the church to the task of reconciliation. But a reconciling community which is itself divided and torn by strife cannot do its work very effectively. It is the realization of this disturbing contradiction in the life of the church that urges so many missionaries, pastors and other Christians to seek for unity in the church, a unity in Christ, a unity in truth and love, which can make the church's proclamation of reconciliation persuasive.

The unity of the church is not necessarily unity of organization, a mammoth ecclesiastical corporation. Nor is unity to be confused with uniformity or regimentation. We are not quite sure what God's gift of unity among the churches will look like, but we hope that it will not mean the loss of any of the Spirit's gifts to the church, nor any lessening of the value of persons. We may suspect that there will be casualties among those things which the church has, sometimes unwittingly, taken over from the society of its time: distinctions of place and rank, elaborate titles and ceremonial, unnecessary distinctions and honors. But everything which enhances the freedom and dignity of the individual, or contributes to the richness and variety of the common life in the body of Christ will, we may hope, be taken up into a more diverse and harmonious unity to the good of the world and the glory of God.

The unity of the church is necessary therefore not as an abstract ideal nor as a matter of administrative efficiency but for the sake of the *mission* of the church. God is at work in the church reconciling men to himself and to each other, redeeming people from their sin and guilt and restoring true integrity to human life in the world. To a splintered, quarrelsome world God offers unity in love in Christ. Unless the church manifests to the world unity in the love of Christ it cannot proclaim its message convincingly or accomplish its work with effectiveness. The overcoming of differences, the elimination of misunderstanding, the reconciliation of the divisions within the church of Christ is desirable so that the church can be what it should be, what it must be if it is to do the work of God in the world.

Movements Toward Unity

The movement to recover the unity of the church, or to give outward expression to the unity which the church has in Jesus Christ, has become an important factor in the world today. It had its beginnings more than sixty years ago in the vision of a few prophetic individuals, in the frustration of missionaries over the disastrous effects of divisions in the church upon the church's mission, and in the impatience of younger churches at the export of divisions along with the gospel. It resulted in three different movements, each in its own way concerned with the unity, renewal and mission of the church. Faith and Order is concerned with discussion of problems of doctrine and church structure, in the hope and confidence that Christians can clear away misunderstandings of each other's tradition, that they can stress what they have in common at least as much as the differences and that they can move toward greater agreement on the points which have divided them. Life and Work explored the possibilities of a common Christian witness, and cooperation in all kinds of common projects, such as education, welfare, help in disaster areas and assistance to younger churches. The International Missionary Council provided a forum and an agency for discussion of the problems of the Christian mission.

When the World Council of Churches was formed in 1948 two of the movements, Faith and Order and Life and Work, became parts of the new organization, and some years later the International Missionary Council also joined forces. Other organizations have made important contributions in the movement toward church unity, especially the YMCA and YWCA and the World Student Christian Federation. These youth groups have provided leadership, enthusiasm and at times a salutary impatience.

It has been said that the most important development in the life of the church today is the ecumenical movement, the growth of concern for the unity of the church. Whether or not this statement is true is not as important as calling attention to the contribution this movement in its many aspects has made to the life of the church. It has undeniably been of great importance so that even those church bodies which have held themselves aloof from the movement have been affected by it in the way they do their theological reflection, in the way they relate to the contemporary world and in the way they understand themselves.

What Has Been Accomplished

What are the contributions of the movement toward unity in this century? First, it has dramatized the problem of disunity, showing what bad effects it has on the life and mission of the church. It has roused interest in seeking Christian unity, and in some circles has stirred hope that the goal can be realized. It has changed the atmosphere of interchurch relations so that discussion is preferred to polemics, and cordially to coolness.

Second, the movement toward unity has helped to lessen misunderstanding between the churches, has reduced the caricatures which used to serve as presentations of another church's position, and has drawn into theological discussion groups which formerly held aloof. Church bodies as widely different as the Orthodox churches and Chilean Pentecostals have been brought together to discuss the problems of theology and mission. All the churches of the west, particularly what may be called old-line denominations, have had their horizons widened by encounter with Greek or Russian Orthodox theologians, brothers from Taizé or representatives of the holiness movements.

Third, it has given the churches a stronger sense of mission to the world. Groups which formerly spoke only of the individual and his inner life have gained a sense of the church as community and the function of this community in the world. Groups whose theological orientation has been primarily to the past have been made aware of the urgency of contemporary problems and have been opened to the possibility that the Holy Spirit calls them to try new ventures of obedience.

Fourth, it has stimulated advances in theological discussion in a number of important areas: the study of Scripture and its relation to tradition, the doctrine of Christ, of the ministry, of Baptism and the Lord's Supper. In some areas it has become clear that the differences which seemed to divide the churches exist also within the individual church bodies, suggesting that if they are not barriers to fellowship within a church body they need not be divisive for denominations either. In at least one area, the doctrine of the Lord's Supper, advances have been made which seem to promise resolution of traditional differences. The statements of the Faith and Order meeting at Edinburgh in 1937 and of the North American Conference of Faith and Order at Oberlin in 1957 show what remarkable agreements have been achieved in this seemingly most difficult area of discussion. More must be said about the convergence on the doctrine of the Lord's Supper in succeeding chapters.

The Contribution of Vatican II

For many years the Roman Catholic church held aloof from the movements toward unity. It offered instead its own program for unity, suggesting that inasmuch as unity could be found only in union with the Bishop of Rome, the way to unity was fairly simple, a return to Rome. Other churches did not surge forward to accept this invitation, but the Roman authorities nevertheless discouraged her priests or members from taking any part in discussions in Faith and Order or other ecumenical agencies. Meanwhile a number of forces were at work within the Roman Catholic church urging a different attitude: students of the

Bible quietly fed the results of historical study of the Scriptures into Catholic theology; the liturgical movement argued the implications of biblical and theological studies for the church's life of worship; a small group of bold and hardy ecumenists worked under discouraging conditions for Roman Catholic participation in ecumenical discussion and for openness to other religious groups; the renewed study of St. Thomas Aquinas brought new insights into dogmatic theology and challenged the prevailing scholastic systems; those concerned with the church's impact upon society urged new viewpoints upon the church in its relation to labor movements, toward democratic societies, toward the world of natural science.

With the accession of Pope John XXIII in 1958 what had been quietly bubbling just below the surface became visible. In January 1959 Pope John called for an ecumenical council and specified that it should deal with questions of Christian unity. To a church and a world which had long assumed that the Vatican Council of 1870 was the last of the councils, this call came as a shock, and no one was quite sure what the council would or could do. The Second Vatican Council convened in the fall of 1962 and met again each fall through 1965. By the middle of the opening session it was apparent that strong forces were at work to establish new relationships with other church bodies, and to rethink many attitudes toward worship, biblical studies, the understanding of the church, the functions of bishops and their relationships to the pope, the relationship of the church to modern society, and to the question of religious freedom. The question was whether these forces were strong and patient enough to overcome the power of the traditionalists, and only in the third and fourth sessions, 1964 and 1965, did it become plain that a majority of bishops had been won over to the views of the progressives and had the acquiescence if not indeed the support of Pope Paul VI.

The Second Vatican Council made dramatic changes in the outlook and practice of the Catholic church, startling to laymen, satisfying to progressives and shattering for traditionalists. The program of the liturgical movement, long resisted and ridiculed, was enacted in the opening fall session. It provided for Mass in the vernacular, revised the liturgy to allow more congregational participation, provided for more exposition of Scripture and appointed a continuing commission to continue revisions of the liturgy, and to prepare a new lectionary of Scripture readings for worship.

The council made major advances in the doctrine of the church, turning away from traditionalist hierarchical and institutional emphasis to stress upon the church as the people of God, upon the priesthood of all believers, on the collegiality of bishops (their sharing with the pope in the responsibility for the administration and mission of the church), and on the universality of the call to holiness. They also in effect settled a long standing argument in the Roman Catholic church about the status of Mary. Theologians had questioned whether Mary should be seen standing with Christ over against the church whether she should be seen rather as a member of the church. After strenuous and sharp debate the bishops voted that a statement about Mary should be included as a chapter in the document of the church. The decision was a disappointment for those who had been hoping for a new Marian dogma; it was encouraging for those within and outside the Roman Catholic church who were concerned with the drawing closer of the churches.

The council's document on the Scriptures was another major contribution to the discussion among the churches. It affirms that the historical-critical study of the Bible is proper and necessary and moves away from the traditional separation between Scripture and tradition by suggesting that tradition consists of the ways in which the message of the Scriptures is handed on from one generation to another. It is no longer a question of Scripture versus tradition but of the traditioning of the scriptural message. This means that discussions with Roman Catholic theologians need not start from the disagreements of the Reformation period but with the questions raised for all the churches by the historical study of the Bible.

Other significant contributions of Vatican II are the Declaration of Religious Freedom, a new statement on relationships with the Jewish communities, the document on the Church and the World Today, and on Missions. But more important than documents is the strong thrust toward rethinking the role of the church in the modern world to overcome the obstacles to Christian unity. In the years following the council the Roman Catholic church has shown remarkable energy in following out these suggestions, sometimes to the dismay not only of conservatives but even of the more cautious progressives.

The combined impact of the movements toward unity among the non-Roman churches and the Second Vatican Council in the Roman Catholic church is to create an almost entirely new situation among the churches, passing by many traditional points of contention and making a new approach to many others. For example, three of the issues controverted so strenuously during the time of the Reformation, justification by grace through faith, the authority of the Scriptures and the priesthood of all believers, are no longer in the center of discussion. Vatican II accepted justification and the priesthood of all believers as biblical teaching, and therefore by their standards Catholic doctrine. In its discussion of the authority of Scripture it accepted the results of historical critical studies and thus confronts the same questions of authority and interpretation that other church bodies wrestle with. The last century has raised questions for all the churches; the new ecumenical situation permits the churches to face them together, studying and listening to the Scriptures together, and listening also to each other as they seek to discern the will of God for the churches in their mission to the world today.

In this discussion among the churches much has already been accomplished. The churches have observed how much they have in common: God, Christ, the Spirit, the Scriptures, the creeds, liturgy, the sacraments, prayer, and note that what is held in common is weightier than what separates. The churches are together in a movement from the defensiveness and polemics of the last century toward a common openness—open to the Scriptures and the voice of the Spirit, open to each other in brotherly counsel and admonition, open to the world as the realm of God's creation and redemption.

II

THE KNOWLEDGE
EXPLOSION
IN HISTORICAL
STUDIES

Reports of progress in overcoming differences between churches are frequently greeted with scepticism by church members. We live, after all, in a world of inflated claims, and people have learned to treat public relations hand-outs with caution. The differences which separate the churches have existed for more than four centuries. If they have proven impossible to overcome in the past, why should they be easier to resolve in our time? And may not the very desire to overcome them be a temptation to church leaders in our pragmatic times? Doctrinal loyalists on both sides suspect that the issues were not squarely faced, or that formulas have been devised to indicate agreement but to conceal real and deep differences, or that one side has simply surrendered to the other.

That movement toward doctrinal agreement is a possibility in our time is due not to the downgrading of theology nor to the skill of theologians in devising deceptive formulas but to transformation of the whole theological enterprise through a tremendous growth in knowledge and through changes in theological perspective. These changes are hardly less momentous than the changes which took place in the natural sciences during the same period, and are just as drastic in their impact upon theological thinking. The growth of historical studies of the Scriptures and of the development of Christian theology and the historical and philosophical study of language itself have been chiefly responsible for these far-reaching alterations of the theological scenery.

The Historical Study of the Bible

The historical-critical study of the Bible has been viewed in many circles with anxiety and suspicion. It seemed improper to treat the Sacred Scriptures with the same kind of critical analysis used on the writings of mere men. When traditional attitudes towards questions of authorship and address were challenged, misgivings were intensified. When traditional doctrines of inspiration, of the work of Christ, of the Lord's Supper were re-examined, shaken up and recast, many thought that they detected the work of the evil one. But over the course of a century the contribution of historical-critical studies is seen to be constructive. It has shaken biblical scholars, but in doing so has compelled them to search the Scriptures more profoundly and listen to the witness of the prophets and apostles more attentively. It has brought new light on familiar passages, shown new relationships among the biblical books, greatly deepened our understanding of almost every theological theme and above all, shown that the Bible has not only one theology but several. The discovery of the variety of biblical theologies has been one of the most far-reaching of all, for it makes it clear that the deed of God in Jesus Christ is so rich in meaning that no one theology can begin to do justice to its complexity and variety. The theology of the New Testament is not a simple solo sung successively by 27 different members of the choir. It is a series of different musical compositions varying greatly in size, richness of theme and elaboration of detail, and giving many different perspectives on the meaning of God's love for man in Jesus Christ.

Some of these theological expositions, especially those of John and Paul are compositions of great complexity, variety of images, insight, subtlety, and evocative power. Others like Matthew, Luke, Hebrews or 1 Peter are less complex, show less imaginative power, but are nonetheless forceful in their presentation of God's work in Jesus Christ.

Varieties of Biblical Theology

The discovery of the almost bewildering variety and complexity of the biblical message has been important for the doctrinal discussions between churches for it suggests that the problem of the theologian is not simply to find the one correct theology and then to discard the others. It is rather that of finding out how the different theologies relate to the variety of biblical theologies, to determine how adequately they expound the apostolic message, and to observe the ways in which the different theologians complete and reinforce each other.

For example, the Lord's Supper has been presented in several different theological patterns in the history of the church. From our tradition of theological argument one might suppose that one of them is right or at least greatly better than the others, and should drive the others out of the church. Examination of these patterns shows, however, that to do so would impoverish the church, for each of them has caught a ray of light from the Scriptures and reflected it so as to illuminate the meaning of the Supper.

1. One pattern has spoken of the Supper as a memorial. It is a dramatic action which reminds Christians of the way God has shown his love in the ministry and death of Jesus Christ. Every time the congregation gathers about this ritual meal it proclaims anew the death of Christ. Calvary and its consequences are experienced again by God's people. The love which called the church into being and which offered itself in death for sinners, reverberates in the life of the gathered people. This is not the whole story of the meaning of the Supper, but any church which excludes this understanding of it is poorer because of it.

2. Another pattern speaks of the Supper as a communion with the crucified, risen, regnant Christ. It is a personal encounter between the living Lord and the needy believer. Jesus Christ gives himself to his people in spite of their unworthiness. He does not simply send a telegram of sympathy, nor mention his friends with a line in his will; he comes to them in the overwhelming but gracious totality of his divine-human life and unites them to himself.

The communion moreover is not simply an encounter

between Christ and the believing individual. He who receives Christ receives the gift of life, and receives that gift in community with other needy humans. The meeting with Christ is also the rediscovery of human community. We are not autonomous persons who wander alone through life; we are members of Christ, of his body the church, sharers in the common life of God's people. The renewal and deepening of our union with Christ is also the re-creation of our fellowship with men. It is a making real and a deepening of a relationship which was given to us in creation, tragically marred by sin, and restored in Christ.

3. Others speak of the Supper as Eucharist or Thanksgiving. The worship of the people of God is here seen as a response to God's approach to us in Christ, and a participation in the true worship which Christ as man offered to God. In our self-centeredness we are unable to worship God in spirit and truth. Our own needs and anxieties always intrude to break our adoration and praise of God. Only by our union with Christ is true worship a possibility for us. As we join with Christ and his people we begin the process of worshipping God as we ought, and in doing so begin to recover the proper dimensions of our humanity. The Supper is therefore both God's gracious address to us in the testimony to the Son who offers himself for his people, and the possibility of our response to this invitation. We can choose to remain in our sin and self-sufficiency and so continue as truncated humans, or we can respond and begin to recover the image of God which is our distinctive endowment as God's creatures. Union with Christ in worship is a school in which we learn the language which distinguishes us from the animals and en-

ables us at least to begin to join in heaven's jubilant praise of God.

4. Another pattern speaks of the Supper as anticipation. Like life in the Spirit, the worship of the church is the reception of the earnest money, our assurance that God is not simply looking at real estate but intends to carry the transaction through to completion. It is tasting the first fruits, the guarantee that the harvest had already begun and that abundant provision lies before us. It is the seal of the signet ring, the impress in the wax which seals the letter and indicates the identity of the sender. The life of the Christian is a life between the ages, with a look backwards in gratitude towards Calvary and a look forward in hope to God's carrying out of his promises. The Supper looks backward to the deed of God which has redeemed us; it looks forward to the act that shall transform us so that we may see him as he is.

5. Another tradition has spoken of the Supper as sacrifice, in language which the Reformation rejected with vehemence. The Reformers opposed language about an unbloody repetition of Calvary offered by the priest on behalf of the people as a sacrifice which gained merit before God. They objected for several reasons: a) they opposed anything which took away the adequacy of Calvary. What Christ did on the cross he did once for all and there can never be need of redoing it. b) They opposed the notion that sacrifice is a movement from man to God. We have nothing to offer God which we have not received from him. The beggar cannot bargain with the king. Moreover the meaning of the Supper is not that we find something to offer to God, but that in Christ he has offered

us the supreme gift, the gift of himself. The Reformers were anxious that there should be no talk of merit, works or offering in the context of man's relation to God. Man deserves nothing; he earns nothing. God gives; man receives, and he receives through God's graciousness.

Nevertheless, what the medieval church was trying to say, and was saying clumsily and with quite inadequate language, is something that should be said, and today, thanks to biblical studies, can be said both more precisely and more powerfully. There is a living connection between the death of Christ understood as sacrifice and the congregation's celebration of the Supper. The New Testament interprets the death of Christ in language borrowed from the cultic or worship language of Israel. Sacrifice is the ritual act by which sinful man is enabled to enter the presence of a holy God. Sacrifice has been understood, and wrongly, as a movement from man to God, a device by which man offers something to God in the expectation that God will do something for him. The deepest meaning of sacrifice is that man offers himself to God; his gift is a sign of his self-giving. But as the prophets untiringly pointed out, man does not really offer himself. In his sinfulness he withholds himself and tries to barter with God, like a bankrupt man trying to purchase an immense estate. But God has instituted sacrifice as a channel of his grace. Men who cannot willingly offer themselves, make offerings which God accepts, not because they are adequate, but because they participate by anticipation in the offering of God's Son for the life of the world. Thus the whole sacrificial system of Israel is understood by the New Testament as a prophetic arrangement, an anticipation of the grace of God to be revealed in

Jesus Christ. Their offerings gain them entry to the presence of God not because of their adequacy as gifts or bribes but through the faith of the worshipper, through his trust in the faithfulness of the God who has promised. Thus in the Old Testament too, justification before God is by grace through faith on the basis of what God is to do in Jesus Christ.

At the end of the sacrificial ritual the worshipper ate a portion of his sacrifice. This was a sign of God's gracious acceptance of the sacrifice and of his invitation to the worshipper to have fellowship at his table. In the Middle East then as today, this was a sign of acceptance as a member of the family and as one entitled to the hospitality, friendship and protection of the host. The meal was the religious climax of the sacrificial ritual. It announced that the man who gave himself to God under the sign of sacrifice, was graciously received by God as a member of his household. The use of sacrificial language in the narrative of the institution of the Lord's Supper, "the body given for you, the blood shed for you," shows how the New Testament interprets Calvary as fulfilment of sacrifice, and the Supper as the ritual meal which assures the worshipper of his gracious reception by God.

The Supper is thus spoken of as sacrifice not in the sense that it repeats Calvary. This cannot be done and should not be spoken of. It is rather the extension of Calvary into the experience of the Christian community: a reminder, a proclamation, a reverberation of Calvary and its benefits. It is not something we offer God. He long ago anticipated us and offered the gift of his Son to us and for us. The Supper thus reminds of the gracious character of the gospel and imparts to believers the benefits of Christ's saving work.

All five of these interpretations of the Lord's Supper have grown up in the church through the study of the Scriptures, and reflection on the meaning of the gospel message for their own times. Each of them has caught something of the teaching of the Bible and expressed it not only in the words of a theological statement but also in a pattern of worship which enables people to experience the realities about which the theology speaks. Each of them has served as a channel for God's blessings to his people. None of them has seen or adequately expressed the entire range of the teaching of the Scriptures concerning the Supper, but all of them understand the Supper as a ritual act in which the most important thing is the action of God moving toward man with his gracious presence. Where the people of God gather with the intention of meeting the risen Christ, remember Calvary (usually by reciting the narrative of Christ's institution of the Supper), and partake of bread and wine in obedience to the command of Christ, there the promise of Christ is fulfilled, and believers have communion with Christ himself in the fulness of his divine-human person. The effectiveness of the Supper as the gift of Christ himself is not dependent upon the theological insight of those who draw near in faith, nor on the liturgical elaboration of the ceremonies, but only upon the faithfulness of God, who has promised and who keeps his promises.

It is important to emphasize this last point, that the Supper is an effectual offer of forgiveness and fellowship because it is an act of God within the Christian community. Theologians sometimes give the impression that the effectiveness of the Supper depends upon the theological precision with which its meaning is formulated or upon the care with which the liturgy is carried out. But since the sacrament is essentially an act of God to be received by faith, people may have confidence that the blessing is actually proffered wherever the sacrament is celebrated provided that three minimum essentials are present: the community's intention to celebrate the sacrament, the reading of the words of promise, and the eating and drinking of bread and wine in obedience to Christ's command. To be sure, good theology is to be preferred to bad, reverent and orderly liturgical practice is better than confusion and disrespect, but it is important to remember that neither theology nor liturgy make the sacrament effectual, but only the faithfulness of God who acts in accordance with his promise.

There are therefore several theologies of the Supper, based on the range of theologies within the Scriptures, which give adequate accounts of what God does as he draws near to men under sacramental signs. None of them exhausts the range of biblical teaching. None of them can drive the others out of the church as false teaching. Each of them should, through study of the Scriptures and attentive listening to the other traditions, seek to deepen its own understanding of the meaning of the Supper so as to channel the riches of scriptural insight into its own exposition and experience of the sacramental reality.

There are theologies of the Supper which are inadequate as expositions of Scripture and of the meaning of the Sacrament. There is more than one way to go wrong in this area. Some deny that the sacrament is an action of God and understand it as a purely human ceremony. This is a fundamental error which fails to grasp the biblical message about God's self-disclosure in Christ and about the coming of Christ to men in the proclamation of the gospel and the use of the sacraments. Some deny that Christ comes to his own people in the sacrament, thinking of sacrament as a rather superficial piece of symbolism. Some contend that it is the faith of the recipient that makes the sacrament, thrusting God out of consideration and leaving man at the mercy of his doubts. However well meant such theologies may be they miss the thrust of the biblical theologies' presentation of the mystery of God's presence in Jesus Christ and in the worship and witness of his church. Their basic error is to overlook the fact that the gospel speaks of a gracious and effectual movement from God to man and not only of man's restless yearnings for deliverance.

Theology Across Denominational Lines

The historical study of the Bible has not destroyed the authority of the Bible. In fact it presents us with a whole complex of biblical theologies more diverse and more profound than any of the church's theological systems. The total spectrum of the church's theological reflection is needed to give an approximation to the variety and power of the biblical interpretation of the mission of Jesus Christ. This situation confronts us with the need for new theological methods, and the abandonment of the old pattern of using polemics to unchurch one's opponents. Out of the experience of the movement toward unity we can discern the outlines of the method of the future:

1. Joint study of the Scriptures that examines it from every possible point of view and explores the full range of its reflection on the gospel.

2. An encounter of theologians in which each listens to the other, not waiting impatiently for an opportunity to refute, but open to the possibility that one's own position may in some respects be inadequate and that one may learn from the representative of another tradition.

3. A search for a common language in which what has been heard from listening to the Scriptures and what has been learned from listening to each other may be formulated with freshness and power. Each of these steps has at least been begun in ecumenical theological discussion during the past half century. The number of persons so far involved is lamentably few and needs to be expanded greatly so that the experience may be more widely shared in the churches.

New Perspectives

Historical studies have not only opened our eyes to the great wealth and variety of biblical theology, but have also given new perspectives on creeds, confessions, and the development of theology. They have thrown much light on problems of theological language, especially concerning the purpose and function of such language, which we shall discuss in the following chapter. They have also enriched our understanding of the Reformers and their time. An older interpretation saw them as great heroes, emphasized their greatness and power, and re-touched the picture so that wrinkles and other blemishes were hardly visible. Historical studies have given the heroic portrait harsh treatment, but it is interesting to note that returning the Reformers to the ranks of human beings has made them more interesting to us and has given us a deeper appreciation of their real achievement. We now see them "warts and all," and while there are certain things in their lives we do not want to praise or defend, we discover that Luther and Calvin, for example, have no need of the efforts of the court painter to prettify them. They loom like giants out of the past and the dimensions of their contribution are clear and impressive.

A New Look at the Confessions

Historical studies have shown us Lutherans that the Augsburg Confession of 1530 is a great theological document which can be appreciated today even by the descendants of its opponents. It is great for one thing because it is truly a *confession*. Those who presented it to the Emperor Charles V found themselves standing before the authorities and confessing their faith in Jesus Christ. The confession does not get lost in incidentals or trivia but focuses on the crucial issues of Christian proclamation. It is great also because it is a *catholic* confession. It is concerned to demonstrate that the Reformers are not heretics, perverters of the truth, mad men bent on de-stroying the church. It affirms the truth of the gospel as it has been handed on in the catholic tradition, avoids novelties and innovations and suggests gently enough that those who have an eye for perversions or innovations can find them in the late medieval tradition. It is great in its *apologetic* character. The Reformers are not arrogant men, at least not here, and they make their case modestly and humbly. They do not ask for the humiliation of their opponents but only for their own right to serve God in the proclamation of his gospel.

The rediscovery of these dimensions of the Augsburg Confession has been valuable to Lutherans in giving a new perspective on priorities. Later theological writing, and even some passages in the later confessions, some-time suggest that the gospel is served first of all in the demolition of other men's theology and that the chief task of theology is polemical, driving the rascals out of the kingdom of God. The Augsburg Confession suggests that the first priority of gospel preaching is the exaltation of Jesus Christ and the pointing of men to that community in which Christ is present and is worshipped. Theology is seen as not primarily polemical, but concerned first of all with the praise of God, with the faithful inter-pretation of the Scriptures as declaring Christ, and with helping people to know themselves as God's creatures, re-deemed and restored to a living hope by the resurrection of Jesus Christ from the dead.

The Reformers, Warts and All

Luther too emerges from historical examination with some bad marks on his report card, but as a great human being nevertheless; a man of profound piety, pastoral compassion, aflame for the glory of Christ, and yet accessible to us because of his humility, his humor, his affection for children, birds and animals and his capacity to laugh at himself. The older heroic portrait conceded that he was not truly a systematic theologian, but the modern portrait challenges that conclusion. Not systematic perhaps in the terms of his contemporary schoolmen, but a systematician in another dimension, one that entitles him to the austere company of Augustine and Thomas Aquinas. He is not concerned with simply resolving dialectical problems, but rather with a picture of God that does justice to the Scriptures and a picture of man that is faithful to the complexity of the human situation as well as to man's paradoxical greatness and misery, made for companionship with the angels but often satisfied to wallow in egocentricity and self-pity.

Other churches have had similar experiences. Calvin has been rediscovered as an excellent interpreter of Scripture, and his theology need no longer be read through the eyes of his immediate successors. The Reformed tradition has been especially enriched through the rediscovery of his theology of the Lord's Supper, which is much closer to Luther's theology than it is to Zwingli's. The confessional tradition of the Reformed church has also been reexamined with the result that Reformed churchmen affirm their confessions in a more catholic or ecumenical way than in the past.

Historical studies have helped Roman Catholics recover the theology of Thomas Aquinas from the bondage of his medieval interpreters. The result has been a simplification and enrichment of Catholic thought. Some Catholic scholars have studied his thought in relation to that of Luther and Calvin and have discovered remarkable areas of agreement in approach to the Scriptures, in presenting the work of Christ, in the understanding of the life of

the Christian and in the doctrine of the Lord's Supper.
The study of the teaching of the Council of Trent has
produced similar surprises, showing that the bishops at
Trent were more careful in defining their positions over
against the Reformers than many of their successors have
been.

III

TRUTH
AND
THEOLOGICAL
LANGUAGE

Another factor in the changing of the theological situation is the study of language. Many different disciplines have contributed to this study, among them linguistics, anthropology, psychology, sociology, medical sciences and several different movements in philosophy. There have been a bewildering number of studies, and it has taken a long time for the various sciences to influence each other and to work toward a common understanding of the problems and facts in the area. The process is still under way, but enough dust has settled to permit a general description of the scene.

It is generally agreed that while man has much in common with the world of animals, he differs from them in some ways, most importantly in his ability to create and use symbolism or language. If we speak of symbolism we should note that there are several kinds of symbolism: language, ritual, mythology, and music. If we prefer to speak of language we should note that in addition to spoken and written language there is also the language of gesture or ritual, that of mythology and that of music. By the use of symbolism or language man is able to remember and interpret his past, to gain a measure of freedom in the present and to anticipate the future either in expectation of happiness or in awareness of the fact of death. Through the powers achieved by use of symbolism human beings have garnered a rich inventory of benefits which we call civilization or culture, and at the same time have produced horrible barbarities and cruelties. Both in his glory and in his shame man differs greatly from the world of animals

One aspect of human language or symbolism is theological language. There are various kinds of theological language, such as that developed by Cicero or the Greek philosophers, or the kind that has grown up in Buddhism or Islam. The theological language used by the Christian community is a special kind, developed in order to speak of what the prophets and apostles regarded as a unique series of encounters with God in the history of Israel and in Jesus Christ. This language is not completely novel: it uses words and syntactical structures which were already at hand. Furthermore, in the history of the church there has been constant interaction between the church's language dealing with the encounter with God in faith, and various other theological languages. This interaction has been the source of enrichment for Christian theology but also the cause of various kinds of confusion, some of which is partly responsible for the tensions existing between church bodies

When Israel met the God of the covenant it began to

separate itself and distinguish itself from the other peoples living in its part of the world. To begin with, it had only the common language of the vegetation religions, those religions concerned to ensure man's survival by enabling him to live in harmony with the powers of the natural world. But Israel had to distinguish its God from the *baalim,* the deities of the vegetation or fertility cults. The Jews used the word god, even though its common meaning referred to one of the many deities of the fertility cults. But they also sought to distinguish their god, by special names or descriptions: the Lord (sometimes rendered Jehovah), the God of Israel, the Lord of hosts, the God of the covenant. Israel's history, at least up to the exile, is the story of the struggle of the prophets to find language and religious practices which would be fitting for the worship and service of the one God, and to avoid confusion with the theology and practices of the other religions. The theology of the covenant, the sacrificial cultus of the temple in Jerusalem, the Sabbath and its customs, the synagogue, the gathering of a body of Scriptures, the tradition of the elders, are all a part of the self-identification of Israel and its attempt to keep its life free of compromises and confusions with the polytheistic religions of the time. Theological language, ritual practices, the disciples of the Torah are all part of the symbolism by which Israel lived out its covenant relationship to God.

The early Christian community was at first a part of the community of Israel, distinguished only by its conviction that the Messiah had come in the crucified and risen Jesus. Christians continued to observe the Torah, worship in the synagogue and temple and to think of themselves as the covenant people. When the implications of their faith in Jesus as Messiah became clearer both to themselves and to the Jewish community a separation took place, assisted by heated arguments over the relationship of Gentiles to the new community. As the mission to the Gentiles gained momentum, the two communities drew farther apart. But the Christian community continued to operate with the vocabulary of Jewish symbolism, theology, worship, a discipline in holiness, each modified to help the young Christian community in its relationship to its Lord.

Theology as Praise of God

In the early church theology had a close connection with worship, evangelism and service. The earliest Christian confession was a very simple one: Jesus is Messiah or Jesus is Lord. The confession had a threefold function: it was an expression of worship and praise, it asserted that Jesus was the fulfilment and true meaning of the prophetic Scriptures, and it served to identify Christians to themselves and to the world. These three aspects, worship or doxology, interpretation of Scripture, and identification of the community, continue to be present in theology through the history of the church, although they undergo change in relative importance and the way in which they are used. The rise of misunderstanding of the gospel and of the person and mission of Christ soon brought about changes in the very form of the confession.

The growth of the simple creed, Jesus is Lord, to the longer Apostles' Creed and the quite complex Nicene or Athanasian creeds shows the struggles of the young

church to clarify the gospel, defend it against misunderstandings, and to preserve the identity of the community
against attempts to change it. Very early in the life of the
church people suggested that Jesus is the revelation of
God and therefore cannot be fully human. The church
replied that Jesus is indeed fully human, completely like
us except for the completeness of his obedience to the
Father. It expanded its confession to include reference
to his genuine humanity: "born of the Virgin Mary,
suffered under Pontius Pilate, crucified, dead, buried."

Others suggested that the assertion of his humanity
was sufficient. To present the obscuring of Jesus' unique
relationship to the Father, the church added to its confession references to his divine sonship: "the only Son
our Lord, conceived by the Holy Spirit." Some theologians sought to emphasize the graciousness of the gospel
by contrasting the love of God in Christ to the wrath of
God in the Old Testament, pushing the point so hard
that some concluded that there are two Gods, a bungling
creator and a gracious redeemer. In reply the church expanded the confession with the addition of a reference
to God the Creator, insisting that the God whom we
meet in Jesus Christ is the same God who created the
universe. One cannot in the name of the gospel drive a
wedge between Christ and the creation. Creation and
redemption are both activities of the one God who wills
the restoration of his creation, not its destruction.

Theology as Interpretation of the Bible

As the church replied to distortions and misunderstandings of the gospel, the doxological function of the-

ology, the praise of God, tended to slip into the background, and the interpretative function became more prominent. Theology is drawn away from the common life of the people of God and becomes the province of the specialist, the theologian. Theology becomes a technical discipline, and both because of the importance of the problems it discusses and because of the fascination with the process of discussion itself, tends to become an end in itself. Instead of seeing theology as a way to clarify the witness to the truth in the gospel, theology is seen as the presentation of the truth itself. At this point theological argument quite easily becomes acrimonious, for if my statement is the presentation of the truth, he who disagrees with it is rejecting not just a form of words, but the truth itself. Then a shift also takes place in the understanding of faith. Faith as response to the gospel or the Word of God gives way to faith as acceptance of theological statements. What started out as a difference over a theological formula has now become heresy and unbelief.

Theology as Identification

The third function of confession also undergoes a change. It continues to serve the Christian community in its self-identification, but a serious if subtle shift has taken place. The early Christian community knew itself first of all through faith in Jesus as Lord. Under the pressure of theological controversy it came to know itself, not so much from its positive affirmation of faith in Christ as from its rejection of misunderstood or distorted confessions, not so much from the Lord it affirms as from the heresies (and heretics) it rejects. When theological controversy becomes heated both sides can easily forget what they have in common: Christ, the church, the Scriptures, the creeds, the liturgy, prayer, a common dedication to holiness. They concentrate rather on what divides them. The more intense the dispute, the easier it is to let relatively unimportant matters destroy fellowship.

The Uses of Theology

The study of language and the historical study of the Scriptures and of doctrine help us to see some characteristics of theology.

1. Theology is a servant, not the master. It is for the sake of the clarity of the gospel and is not an end in itself. Just as complicated automobiles create a demand for skilled mechanics, so theological problems call for competent theologians. But the purpose of the engine is to propel the automobile, and only incidentally for the improved economic status of the mechanic. The purpose of theology is to keep faith focused on Jesus Christ and to indicate the importance of other things in relation to him. Theology ought to be closely related to the church's life of worship, to its attempt to witness to Christ in its proclamation and to the church's service to the world. It should not become a private game for theologians, nor should it distort worship, witness and service because of the private academic interests of theologians.

Theology helps worship by its study of what Christian worship ought to be, by its examination of the present worship life of the church and by suggesting patterns of worship to help the church to become more effectively the people of God. Theology serves witness through its interpretation of the Scriptures, its study of the creeds and confessions of the church and by its suggestion of language and activities which placard Jesus Christ as Lord to the men of today. It assists the church's life of service by its knowledge of past patterns of service, its awareness of the needs of people and society today and by its insight into ways in which the love of God can become flesh in the church's self-giving for the life of the world.

2. Theology is a witness to the truth; it is not the truth itself or the container for the truth. For the Scriptures truth belongs to God alone and is accessible to humans only as God discloses it to them. The Fourth Gospel asserts that Jesus Christ is himself the truth, and that the truth is known by faith, that is, the believing response to God's offer of life in the gospel. Ephesians also uses the strange phrase "as truth is in Jesus," which may parallel the suggestion of the Fourth Gospel that God has revealed the truth in Jesus Christ and that faith is the way man apprehends it. The truth of God lies beyond any and all theological statements. It is to be found in him through whom God speaks his decisive word to us all. Knowledge of the truth is by the double movement of repentance and faith, in which we set aside our own aspirations to divinity and accept the sovereignty of God in Christ.

The purpose of theology is therefore to help keep things in focus so that the church holds forth Jesus Christ with clarity and power, and does not permit anything to obscure him. It must be conceded that often enough theology has not done this well. It has at times served as attorney for the vested interests of the institutional church; it has permitted the smoke of its controversies to obscure the name of Christ; it has sometimes forgotten the poor and uneducated and sought to feed them not with the Word of God but with theological tomes. But the continued voice of the gospel in the church also reminds us that theology has sometimes done its work adequately and its clear proclamation of the gospel brings joy to many.

3. Theology has a protective or interpretative function. Its task is to phrase the church's message so as to protect the mystery of God's redeeming presence among men from misunderstanding, distortion or watering down. The church does not do much on its own, nor need it do so. Its function is to serve as a channel through which God can bring his blessings to men. It is at its best when it gets out of the way so that the work of God can go forward in its midst. It is the business of theology to help the church be where God can do his work, and to avoid cluttering the landscape with piously intended obstructions.

In this task of protection or interpretation theology frequently finds itself compelled to use language which seems self-contradictory. It found itself so bound to assert that Jesus Christ is truly human, completely one of us except that his humanity is unmarred by disobedience to the Father. It also asserted that Jesus is the unique Son of God, that in him the fulness of the Godhead dwelled in a bodily form. By standards of human logic it is possible to say one or the other of these propositions, but to assert both is a threat to reason. It is not that the theologians have fallen in love with contradictory language, but that they find themselves compelled by their reflection on the life and ministry of Jesus Christ and by the scriptural testimony to it to affirm things that strain language to the breaking point. To affirm only one side would be unfaithful; in spite of the threat to logical consistency they find themselves bound to assert both.

The language of theology, like the language of the Bible, is ordinary human language pressed into the service of a most extraordinary message. The prophets found their vocabulary in a most unpromising place, in the fertility religions of the ancient Near East. But while making use of this language they found ways to express the distinctiveness of their message. When the temple was constructed it was based on models derived from Near Eastern religious practices. But the builders of the temple in Jerusalem found ways to assert the distinctive prophetic message nevertheless. The shrine, for example, had no image of the covenant God. Instead they placed within the sanctuary the ark of the covenant, the tables of the law, Aaron's rod and a pot of manna, reminders all of the deeds of God in delivering his people from bondage and giving them a land to dwell in. The writers of the Bible find their language where they can, borrowing any term or image that serves their purpose, but finding ways to challenge the religious ideas of the world from which they took their language in order to testify to the unique majesty and love of their God.

Theories of inspiration sometimes give the impression that the Bible glided from heaven to earth untouched by human hand. But examination of the Bible itself and comparison with the world out of which it came, show that the prophets and apostles used the language of the world about them. They often changed its meaning by putting it into different relationships or contexts, as when material from a Babylonian epic is used in the creation narrative in Genesis, or ideas from dualistic Persian religion are torn down out of their dualistic context to speak of a dramatic conflict between God and the forces of evil.

All languages have a number of words which identify what we might call the furniture of human life. We have agreed on conventional terms to describe the common artifacts of human life: houses, dishes, clothing, food, elemental human relationships. But whenever we want to go beyond these conventional terms we are driven to the use of metaphor. Metaphorical, pictorial or symbolic language thus becomes the vehicle for most of the more subtle or important matters in human life. Literalist language has its limitations; it is flat-footed and cannot leap or soar. When therefore we want to go beyond groceries and brooms we must make use of metaphor.

Theology and Metaphor

Biblical language used the agreed conventions for naming houses, roads and parts of the body. But when it moves to unfolding the meaning of the life and ministry of Jesus Christ it resorts to metaphors, many of them familiar from the writings of the prophets, some of them drawn from the Gentile world about them. They borrow from the language of the temple to speak of Christ's work as sacrifice, from the language of the slave market to picture it as redemption, from the strains of married life to picture it as reconciliation. The Bible is a huge gallery of these pictures used by the prophets and apostles to portray what literal or furniture language is unable to express.

The language of the Bible has more in common with great poetry than it has with a book of instructions for the operation of a calculating machine. When language fails us in our speech about the important matters of life, it is to poetry that we turn to make our point. We strain language to the breaking point, and sometimes even then are unable to communicate what we wish to say. Then we can understand the psalmist who finding no adequate language to praise God's goodness urges, "taste and see that the Lord is gracious." There is a point where language breaks down and we can only urge that our hearers try it for themselves in order to experience the love and mercy of God.

The Bible therefore speaks of God not in abstract philosophical language but in pictures: God is Father, king, shepherd, farmer, victorious general, bridegroom, the host at the feast. Israel is seen correspondingly as a wayward son, a rebellious subject, a lost sheep, a fruitless field or vineyard, an adulterous bride, and a reluctant guest at the wedding. God's activity in redeeming his people is intended to gain the obedience of his son, win the loyalty of his rebellious subjects, recover his lost sheep, care patiently for the vineyard until it bears fruit, recover the love of his bride and have a wedding celebration crowded with guests.

The writers of the Scripture are content to use pictorial language. Scientists and philosophers, however, have not been satisfied with it and have worked strenuously to develop a language with precise meanings, so that communication can be as exact as possible. This kind of language is possible in mathematics, and the attraction of mathematical language has been strong to philosophers and theologians. The language of metaphor and poetry seems too vague and imprecise, too emotional to do a clear job of communicating. Poets are acceptable in the parlor after dinner, where people can relax and enjoy language which has emotional overtones. But they do not belong in philosophical discussion, for their words have too many fuzzy edges to be precise, and they interfere with the cool exactness needed for serious matters.

The modern study of language has shown that exactness of speech and the avoidance of metaphor is possible in a few disciplines, such as mathematics and the physical sciences, but not attainable in disciplines dealing with relationships among humans. Students in these fields have often supposed that they have achieved a language without metaphors, but most often they have done it by overlooking the metaphor or concealing it in a word of foreign origin. Psychologists, for example, speak of repressions. Here a word of Latin origin conceals the metaphor of pushing back. Or they may speak of censors operating on the material of dreams. Again a Latin word conceals a Roman official who sits at the threshold of the dream experience.

Theologians have also supposed that their words were scientifically exact terms, with all metaphorical elements eliminated. But reconciliation remains a metaphor for patching up a quarrel, redemption a metaphor for buying the freedom of a slave, and other apparent abstractions, metaphors whose pictorial character has been forgotten. Theological work has often obscured the message of the Scriptures by taking biblical metaphors and expounding them in apparently abstract terms. The task of preaching then becomes one of finding appropriate illustrations to make the theological abstractions accessible to ordinary people again. Modern linguistic studies would seem to suggest that theology would be improved by the elimination of the middle man. If the metaphors of the Bible can be expounded as metaphors they touch human life at many points and evoke insight from anyone who can use language at all. The preacher can be spared part of his industrious quest for illustrations, for they are built into the biblical text and need only to be liberated by interpretation. The Bible, though still a complex and difficult book, becomes more accessible to ordinary persons and speaks simply and with power.

The study of language has removed some of the pretensions of theology, taking away its claim to be the truth or to present truths and showing it to be symbols or signs pointing to the truth which is in Jesus Christ. It enables us to see that all theologies, to the extent that they really wrestle with the fact of Christ, are talking about realities and experiences common to all Christians. However much they may differ in language or method, they are attempts to expound the mystery of God's gift of life in Christ. By emphasizing the differences we can get the impression that the various theologies are quite different and that they cannot be reconciled to each other. But by stressing their attempt to expound the meaning of Christ and his mission for men we discover that they have much in common and that their differences are not contradictions of each other, but the contribution of different instruments to the full orchestration of God's praise. In this way they do not try to destroy each other but rather help each other become more eloquent in describing the mighty deeds of him who has called us from darkness into his marvelous light.

IV

THE REFORMED CHURCHES: AGREEMENT ON GOSPEL AND SACRAMENTS

The Lutheran and Reformed churches are in many ways very close together. They have a common allegiance to the Scriptures, agree that the message of justification by grace alone through faith is the heart of the gospel, stress the priesthood of all believers, and hold similar views on most of the points at issue between the Roman Catholic church and the Reformers. Yet these two churches have been unable to declare fellowship with each other, implying that each finds the other seriously defective in its presentation of the Christian message. What are the issues which have kept them apart through more than four centuries?

The Roots of Disagreement

For Lutherans the chief issue has been the doctrine of the Lord's Supper. They have contended that the Reformed tradition is not fully scriptural in its interpretation of the sacrament, that it sees the sacrament chiefly as something men do and denies that Jesus Christ comes to believers with the fullness of his redeeming presence. This raises for Lutherans further questions as to how Reformed churches understand God's movement toward man in Jesus Christ. They have suspected that Reformed theologians, despite the splendid way in which they speak of the grace of God, the sinfulness of man, the importance of faith, the presence and power of the Holy Spirit, fail nevertheless to take with full seriousness the biblical message about the revelation of God in Christ and the continued self-giving of God to sinners in the preaching of the gospel and the celebration of the sacraments.

This general attitude of wariness and suspicion has led Lutheran theologians to examine each item of Reformed doctrine with a magnifying glass and has led to the conclusion that Reformed doctrine is seriously defective in at least three other areas: the doctrine of Christ, the doctrine of predestination, and in the understanding of the way. Christ's kingship is expressed in the world. The discussion between the two traditions on these issues has been long, heated and at times bitter. It has led some theologians with a passion for thoroughness to such caustic evaluation of the other tradition that one wonders how Christ could be known or worshipped through its ministrations.

Lutheran theologians in their discussion of the Lord's Supper have stressed the gracious condescension of God to sinners. It is one of the wonders of his mercy that he steps down to the level of sinners and has fellowship with them. He does not insist that sinners shall earn acceptance in heaven as a prerequisite for fellowship. Nor does he merely offer a compromise and promise to come down part way if only man will goad himself into moving part way up. He recognizes the plight of man as a sinner, sees his inability to help himself and therefore offers fellowship on the basis of sin confessed and repented. He who accepts this astonishing offer is accepted by God for the sake of what Jesus Christ has done and becomes a member of God's family, not simply a slave, or a servant, but a son.

Lutherans found Zwingli's theology of the Supper unsatisfactory at this point. Zwingli found talk about the presence of Christ in the Supper to be materialistic and superstitious, and insisted that the meaning of the Supper is symbolic: it reminds the congregation of what God has done in the cross of Christ, and thus calls to mind the gospel and the grace of God. But Christ is not present among the congregation in the celebration of the Supper. He is in heaven, at the right hand of God, and even in his glorified body is limited to this one place. Therefore to speak of Christ being present under bread and wine is to indulge in superstitious talk, which is not fitting for Christians.

John Calvin speaks of Christ's presence in the Supper as *real* and *spiritual*. The word *real* seeks to assert the traditional Christian teaching about the Supper: Christ is present for those who have faith, and imparts to them the benefits of his death and resurrection. What is received under the sign of bread and wine is Christ himself. This is the way he has chosen to confirm to his people the forgiveness of sins. The word *spiritual* insists that Christ is present in a spiritual way: that is to faith, by the work

of the Holy Spirit, in accordance with the promise of
the gospel. His presence is not something which can be
felt with the tongue. The bread remains bread and the
wine, wine. They are not transformed by some miracle
into the actual physical body and blood of Christ, but are
the sacramental signs of Christ's presence in accordance
with his promise. Had Calvin said no more than this his
teaching might have been acceptable to Lutherans, but he
went on to say more.

Calvin was convinced that the union of God with man
in the person of Jesus Christ was a complete and permanent relationship. Jesus Christ the risen one still has a
human body, but one glorified through his resurrection
and ascension. Even in the glorified state, however, it
continues to have the characteristic of human bodies in
that it can be in only one place at a time. Therefore
Christ's presence in the Supper is a presence outside of
the flesh. Calvin can also speak of a communion with
Christ in heaven through the work of the Holy Spirit.
Calvin's problem was to reconcile his quite sound conviction that the union of God and man in Jesus Christ is
permanent and intimate (and not merely a passing encounter like a bird roosting on a branch) with his view
of the world derived from pre-Copernican models. For
the Lutherans his solution seemed too much akin to Zwinglian ideas and a threat to God's condescension in drawing
near to sinners.

The Doctrine of Christ

Suspicious of Calvin's theology of the Supper, the
Lutherans began to question his doctrine of Christ also.

They were convinced that his idea of a presence of Christ outside of the flesh reflected an inadequate view of the unity of the person of Christ and of the communion of human and divine qualities or attributes in his person. Calvinists said that the human is incapable of sharing divine attributes. The Lutherans maintained that it was, and thus Christ could be present everywhere not just in his divinity, but also in his glorified humanity.

This whole argument seems to us unreal and artificial, for to us the difference between earth and heaven is more than a difference in distance or space. We can know something about earth, but our speech about heaven is a projection of earthly images or analogies, and we are not at all confident that heaven corresponds to the models we make of it. We are more edified by Luther's approach to this problem. He simply refuses to think of the expression "right hand of God" in spatial terms. He regards it as a pictorial expression for the power of God. To speak of Christ sitting at the right hand of God is not an attempt to locate Christ in space but an assertion that the risen Christ shares in the exercise of God's power in the world. The attempt to explain how Christ is present in the Supper is impossible and fruitless, as Luther recognized, although he himself attempts to do something of the sort in his discussions with Zwingli about the ubiquity of Christ.

Predestination

The Lutheran objection to the Calvinistic doctrine of double predestination is that it conflicts with the biblical insistence that the grace of God is meant for all men.

If God from eternity decrees that some shall be saved and others lost, the gospel is not really addressed to the latter group. It is a genuine offer of life only to those destined to salvation; for the others it is a cruel deception. Calvin himself regarded the doctrine as "a terrible decree," but from his reading of Romans 9-11 considered it a biblical teaching and therefore binding upon the church. The majority of Calvinists in modern times agree with Calvin that it is a terrible decree, but disagree that it is demanded by the interpretation of Romans or other parts of Scripture.

The Calvinists had their own suspicions about the Lutheran understanding of the Supper and of the doctrine of Christ which lay behind it. When Lutherans reacted warily to talk of a spiritual presence this seemed to Calvinists a suggestion that Lutherans were guilty of materialism and superstition, and did not in fact really differ from the Roman-Catholics. Calvinists suspected a concealed doctrine of transubstantiation (the teaching that the bread and wine cease to be bread and wine in the Supper and are transformed into the body and blood of Christ. Of this more must be said in Chapter 6). They accused Lutherans of Capernaitic eating, an expression suggested by John 6:52: "How can this man give us his flesh to eat." Lutherans on their part insisted that the presence is not material, or spatial, or spiritual, but sacramental, that is, a kind of presence unique to the Lord's Supper.

The Lutheran doctrine of the person of Christ came under fire from the Reformed in the same way. If the sacramental theology is coarse and materialistic, so must be also the doctrine of Christ. The insistence that the risen Christ can be present at many different places at the same time because the humanity can share the divine quality of omnipresence sounded to Reformed theologians like the ancient heresy of Eutychianism, a doctrine which suggested that the humanity of Jesus is absorbed into his divinity.

The Kingship of Christ

Lutherans and Reformed have followed different patterns of thought on the way Christ makes his impact upon the world. The Calvinists followed the line of the Middle Ages and spoke of the kingship of Christ. Since his resurrection and glorification Christ is king of the universe, and exercises his kingship through the church. Roman Catholics of this time thought of the church as the institutional church under the rule of the hierarchy, and made strong claims about the church's right to seat and unseat kings. Calvinists thought of the church as the body of elect believers through whom Christ extended his reign, among believers by the gospel, among non-believers through the law. The church has therefore the double task of preaching the gospel so that Christ may be received in faith, and of urging upon all men obedience to the law of God.

Lutherans spoke of two realms over which Christ reigns as king, the realm of creation where Christ is Lord but hidden, and the realm of grace where Christ is Lord and revealed as such to faith. Christ is Lord of the entire creation, but is revealed as Lord only in the Gospel, only to believers. As creator he works in the world in a hidden way, using the structures of the creation to nudge the world toward purposes of his own which are revealed in the gospel. The chief function of the church is to preach the gospel, and to use the law of God to drive men to repentance and faith. The church must recognize that Christ is at work also in the world, in the political authority, in the family, in the various ways in which people are dependent upon each other. The church must not attempt to do the work of the political authority, or to prevent the proper authority from doing its job. But it does have the responsibility to interpret the law of God to those who have power, lest they think the power is their own, and forget the God who has created them and put them in a position of authority.

The danger attending the kingship of Christ approach is that men forget that Christ is king and execute his will over-confidently and with arrogance. This was the temptation of the medieval church, and modern churches have not been entirely exempt from it.

The danger of the two realms approach is that the realms may be separated rather than distinguished, with several possible results. Christ's kingship over the creation may be forgotten and the creation ceded to political authorities, commercial exploiters, or to the devil himself. Christ's kingship over the creation may be misunderstood as unqualified approval of everything in the world, a theology of culture which leaves the church no prophetic function to perform. Or the church may pay lip service to Christ's lordship in the world but concentrate upon a piety of inwardness which leaves the church in mystical contemplation while any one who wants to can run off with the world.

When Differences Are Not Divisive

Theological conversations between Reformed and Lutheran theologians have taken place recently both in North America and in Europe. Between 1963 and 1966 representatives of most Reformed and Lutheran bodies in North America met to discuss traditional theological differences on the doctrine of Christ, the Lord's Supper, and law and gospel. They concluded in 1966 with a declaration that each group recognized in the other's teaching a common understanding of the gospel, and that while many doctrinal differences still existed they were not of a kind to be obstacles to mutual understanding and fellowship. They also recommended that the "churches enter into discussions looking forward to intercommunion and the fuller recognition of one another's ministries."

Because of problems in both groups of churches, Presbyterian involvement in the Consultation on Church Union and on the Lutheran side attempts to overcome divisions within American Lutheranism, this recommendation did not call forth immediate action. Not until 1972 did the conversations requested by the resolution get under way. In the meantime conversations between Reformed and Lutheran theologians were carried on in Europe, involving representatives from almost all European countries, and climaxing in the Leuenberg Agreement of 1972. This agreement represented several years of work by a cross section of European theologians and has been referred to the various Reformed and Lutheran churches in Europe for discussion. Several churches have already indicated their approval of the agreement and it appears likely that most of them will do so.

What is the course of the discussion which has moved Reformed and Lutheran theologians from centuries of disagreement to a declaration that the differences which exist are not divisive?

The great problems facing the modern world no doubt have something to do with it, at least in preparation of an atmosphere of urgency. The momentum of the movement for the recovery of unity has also contributed much, especially a spirit of cordiality and of confidence that at least some traditional disagreements can be overcome. But had not the theological situation undergone great changes it is doubtful that these combined influences could have accomplished much. In the 16th century the very existence of the Reformation churches seemed to depend upon agreements among the churches, yet the churches remained in conflict, all convinced that they were contending for the truth.

Biblical studies have made the major contribution. The discovery of the different theologies of the Bible opened theologians to the possibility of theologies which differ but complement each other rather than contradict or oppose each other. The realization that the New Testament interprets the Lord's Supper in a variety of images led to the awareness that no church's theology exhausted the riches of the meaning of the Supper, or corresponded to the full spectrum of biblical interpretations of it. Every church is confronted by the task of enriching its own sacramental theology in order to do justice to the Scriptures, and by the need to acknowledge the insights of other churchly traditions as biblically grounded. This had led to a new appreciation of the function of the Lord's Supper in the life of the congregation and an increased sensitivity to the pain and scandal of refusing fellowship at the Lord's Table to other Christians. Above all it has become clear that the Supper is not primarily an act of men, but an act of God who gives himself to his people, and in so doing reconciles, empowers and renews his church.

The impact of biblical studies has of course reached far beyond Lutheran and Reformed churches, bringing about changes in sacramental thinking all the way from Roman Catholicism to the free churches and charismatic groups. The wide spread rediscovery of sacrament as God's action in the Christian community has given a new sense of the presence of Christ in the community, in the preaching of the Word of God, and in the sacraments. It has provided new ways of speaking of the Supper which can stress God's work in the sacraments without being suspected of materialism or magic. The Statement on the Lord's Supper adopted at the North American Conference on Faith and Order at Oberlin in 1957 shows how far this kind of thinking has penetrated into American Protestantism. In the light of these great changes, the stereotypes used in traditional theological handbooks need careful reexamination.

Historical studies in theology have also made a notable contribution toward the new convergence of the churches. Lutherans have rediscovered Martin Luther and found in him a theology richer, warmer, more personal and more catholic than that of their theological handbooks. It has become clear that there is more in Luther than an insistence on the real presence and the rejection of transsubstantiation and of Zwingli. The roots of his teaching in the Scriptures, in the ancient fathers and in the mystical theology of the Middle Ages were seen in more detail, showing his kinship to certain theological streams in the Orthodox churches and in Roman Catholicism.

The rediscovery of John Calvin has been equally momentous for the Reformed churches. He too was seen as deeper and more subtle than the traditional handbooks had shown. His teaching on the Lord's Supper was seen to be a fuller exposition of the Scriptures than that of Zwingli, whose teaching on the Supper had been adopted by many Reformed churches. This displacement of Zwinglianism, because of the impact of biblical theology and of Calvin's theology, has restored to some Reformed churches an understanding of the sacrament as God's act in the church and of the role of the Supper as renewer of unity among the people of God, unity with Christ, with each other, and with all Christians.

When Reformed and Lutheran theologians meet today to discuss the Lord's Supper they find themselves in a new situation. Both sides have penetrated more deeply into the Scriptures and are aware of the plurality of biblical theologies. Both sides have new perspectives on their own confessional tradition and have relinquished some of their stereotyped versions of the theology of the other side. Both can now acknowledge that where sacrament is seen as a work of God, a variety of interpretations of that work is both legitimate and necessary. They can therefore acknowledge what in the other tradition is rooted in the Scriptures, listen together to the Scriptures for new insight into the meaning of Christ's work, learn from the other tradition, and together seek new language to present the riches of the Christian message more persuasively to men of our time. The differences that exist between the traditions are no longer seen as divisive, but as invitations to a broader and deeper understanding of the meaning of the sacrament.

In the discussion of the doctrine of Christ a similar development has taken place. No longer is it necessary to demonstrate that the doctrine of the other church is grossly inadequate or heretical. Each tradition has mined the Scriptures and the writings of the fathers and stands in agreement with the traditional doctrine of Christ expressed in the great ecumenical creeds. But we now understand the great creeds not as chemical formulas showing us how to reconstitute the person of Christ, but rather as attempts to protect the mystery of God's presence and work in Christ from misunderstandings and distortions. This protective or explanatory function of the creeds leads to verbal fence building and there are fences on each side that have been under attack. So it is necessary to say that Jesus is fully human, more fully human than we are, because he lives in complete fellowship with God. But we must also say that Jesus has a unique relationship to God, is the Son of God, the revelation of God. We must say, moreover, that the life he lived was the life of a fully human being, not divided into divine and human compartments, or acting now as God, now as man.

In the handing on of this Christian tradition Reformed theologians have been concerned to stress the sovereignty of God and the "infinite qualitative difference" between God and man. Their teaching seeks to preserve the majesty and the grace of God against human presumption. Man is always the object of God's grace. Even in his union with Christ he remains the creature. He may be designated a son of God, but never because of his own natural capacities. His status is due to God's fathomless mercy. The sobriety of the Reformed doctrine of Christ is an enduring defence against human pride, against romantic ideas of what union with Christ means and against man's constant tendency to deify himself.

Lutherans have highlighted the movement of God toward men, his mercy and condescension and the genuineness of God's work among men. Man is indeed a sinner; he deserves nothing but judgment: at no time does he have any claim on God save that of God's promise. But God did not simply make a gesture toward his creatures, he accomplished something. In Jesus Christ he gave the new humanity, a genuinely human life which we can share through our union with him. God did not simply talk about community: In Jesus Christ he created the new community, his new people in the world. The sacrament is not simply a love letter; it is the bestowal of Christ himself, the warrant that God means business, that the new creation is already in existence. The Lutheran doctrine of Christ opposes all attempts at minimizing the reality of God's work in Christ, whether by turning it into pious talk, or by forgetting that the world is God's creation, or by postponing everything really Christian until the day of judgment.

Reformed and Lutheran theologians have thus discovered each other within the ample boundaries of the traditional Christian witness to Christ. They can recognize each other as fully Christian and orthodox. In the new mood of chastened realism, they can recognize that both traditions have their achievements and their tragedies. They can therefore listen to each other the more readily hoping to learn from each other and in common theological work to produce a witness to Christ for today which is more convincing and persuasive than anything either tradition has been able to do.

When the questions concerning Christ and the Lord's Supper have been examined in the new perspectives given by historical study, other problems appear in a different light also. The doctrine of double predestination, which has been the cause of much controversy, was not even on the agenda in the North American Reformed-Lutheran conversations in 1963-66. This is partly because the Calvin revival has shown the doctrine in a different perspective, but mainly because Calvinists have themselves modified their theology at this point, rejecting any teaching of predestination which limits the scope of God's grace.

The European conversations discussed predestination and came to the agreement that election can be discussed only in connection with "the invitation to salvation in Christ," that the gospel promises "God's unconditional acceptance of sinful man," and that "the witness of Scripture forbids us to suppose that God has uttered an eternal decree for the definite condemnation of specific persons." It concludes that "where such agreement exists, the earlier judgments concerning the doctrine of predestination no longer have any object."

The problems of law and gospel and of social ethics were discussed in the American conversations and differences of theological approach and style were noted, as well as the different use of terms such as law. The areas of agreement are greater than they were in the 16th century and both groups can acknowledge that their doctrinal statements are inadequate in certain ways, in limiting the scope of redemption to men, for example, and losing sight of God's redemptive purpose for his whole creation. That differences still exist is clear, but the differences are those that can and should exist within the one community of Christ. Differences are necessary if we are to be challenged to reflection and to reexamination of our proclamation. It is only when they falsify the gospel or obscure the glory of Christ that they are a danger to the church.

The European conversations did not discuss the problems of law and gospel because they did not regard the Reformed and Lutheran positions as excluding each other. They acknowledge that these differences, like those regarding forms of worship, types of spirituality and church order, may be deeply felt by congregations, but that by the standards of the New Testament and the Reformation they should cause no separation among the churches. These differences should, however, be the subject of continuing discussion among the churches so that the common understanding of the gospel on which fellowship is based may be further deepened and tested.

What will result from the Reformed-Lutheran conversations in Europe and America?

It appears that a majority of the European churches who have been represented in the Leuenberg discussions will approve the agreements, and in doing so declare that they are in pulpit and altar fellowship with the other churches who have endorsed them. This means that they recognize the other churches as the church of Jesus Christ, acknowledge their ministries as being fully Christian ministries, and admit their members to communion. After the mutual denunciations of the past this will mean a new era in the relationships of the churches, opening up new possibilities. Some churches may hesitate to endorse the agreements out of anxiety at taking so unfamiliar a course, and fear of the kind of development that may follow opening up their homes to so many strange people.

At this stage the agreements mean no more than the declaration of fellowship, important as this is to the removal of scandal from the life of Christ's church. It does not mean that church unions must be negotiated within a certain time. There are no doubt situations where churches should join together to enhance their Christian witness and to strengthen each other. In other situations the churches may wish to become accustomed to so novel a relationship, and to wait upon the results of their new association to see what course is right for the future. Those who fear a general amalgamation into one immense ecclesiastical corporation should know that few people active in interchurch discussion today have much taste for such huge complexes, but prefer to contemplate the growth of fellowship and cooperation amid all the diversity that now characterizes the scattered churches of Christ.

The declaration of fellowship implies a commitment to further the unity so recognized by future cooperation of various kinds, in theology, worship, in missions, evangelism, welfare services, social ethics, education. No gift of the Spirit should be given up; no weakness or abuse should go unchallenged. We do not know what the Spirit wills for us in the future, except that we should respond to him step by step as he confronts us with needs and responsibilities.

V

THE ANGLICANS: THE NEED FOR NEW METHODS

The Lutheran churches of East Africa and India are responsible for the opening of conversations between Anglicans and Lutherans. Discussions looking toward a union of a number of churches had begun in both regions, and it soon became apparent that Anglican and Lutheran approaches to the question of unity were quite different. The Lutheran World Federation was requested by its member churches in East Africa and India to enter into conversations in order to clarify differences and if possible to resolve them. The request was endorsed by the Federation's commissions on World Missions and Theology and in 1967 the executive committee of the Federation voted to establish contacts. Once begun, negotiations moved rapidly, and in 1968 the Lambeth Conference of the Anglican Communion and the Executive Committee of the Lutheran World Federation authorized appointment of a representative Anglican-Lutheran Commission. The following year a similar group representing American Episcopalians and Lutherans began conversations with very cautiously defined goals. They were instructed to explore the possibilities of a more extended conversation with more specific goals of fellowship or unity. Both groups completed their assigned tasks in 1972 and reported back to those who had appointed them. The results of both discussions are to be published very soon after the appearance of this account.

So Much in Common

Anglicans and Lutherans have much in common, as the groups taking part in the discussions discovered. They also have quite different approaches to a variety of problems in theology, worship, church polity and Christian ethics. It is this interesting combination of things held in common, but understood or interpreted in widely different ways, that made Anglican-Lutheran conversations both difficult and rewarding.

Let us look first at the common elements.

1. Both churches look to the Scriptures as the norm for their teaching and practice. They have a similar range of attitudes, both in the recognition of the authority of Scripture and in the acceptance of historical-critical studies as a necessary part of the process of interpretation. The differences which exist are not between the churches but between groups in both churches, between those who accept with varying degrees of enthusiasm the historical approach to the study of the Bible and those who look at critical studies with suspicion or disapproval.

2. Both churches esteem the ancient creeds, the Apostles' and the Nicene, as authoritative statements of doctrine, refer to them frequently in their theological study and use them in the worship of the congregations.

3. Both churches have confessions, doctrinal statements developed during the period of the Reformation, although there are wide differences in the authority which is ascribed to them and the use made of them in theology and in the life of the congregations. Both churches affirm the doctrine of justification by grace through faith as a basic theological insight in the church and as a key to the interpretation of the Scriptures. The way the doctrine is worked out in the life of the church varies greatly in the two communions.

4. Both churches practice baptism as a rite of initiation into the Christian community, and insist that instruction in the faith must be closely connected with the practice of the sacrament. Both agree that while infant baptism is not clearly attested in the Scriptures as a practice of the first century church, it is a very ancient usage and is consonant with biblical teaching wherever instruction in the faith is conscientiously undertaken by the congregation and parents.

5. Both churches have a rite of confirmation, in which, after a period of instruction, those who desire to be confirmed in their Christian faith are commended to God with the laying-on of hands and prayer for the guidance and power of the Holy Spirit. The meaning of confirmation and its relation to baptism are being studied in both churches and both have begun the practice of admitting persons to the Lord's Supper before confirmation.

6.   Both churches esteem the preaching of the Word of God, use liturgies which are remarkably alike, emphasize strongly the importance of the Lord's Supper, and agree in many particulars of interpreting the meaning of the Supper for the life of the congregations. Both have tended to interpret fellowship in the Supper as the sign of a unity which exists rather than as a means of achieving such unity. The churches resemble each other strongly in their preservation of traditional forms of worship, including liturgies, Scripture lessons, vestments, church furnishings and music.

7.   Both churches agree that relationship to Christ is the link which binds the contemporary church to the church of the apostles. Both are concerned to be apostolic, that is, genuinely sent forth to mission by Christ, and to have an apostolic ministry. This point of agreement is however also the point at which different approaches to the life of the church become clear. They agree on the necessity of an apostolic ministry, but seek to preserve apostolicity in quite different ways.

What Does It Mean to Be Apostolic?

Anglicans have found in their experience that the traditional office of bishops is of great value in preserving the apostolic character of the church. They accordingly tend to test the apostolicity of other communions by the same signs which have proven so valuable in their own history. They have a sense of familiarity in approaching churches as different as the Orthodox, Roman-Catholics, or Old Catholics because they too have bishops in the traditional pattern. They are able to understand Swedish and Finnish

Lutherans and their spiritual descendants in the third world. But they are puzzled by other Lutherans, some of whom have bishops with no claim to a lineal succession from the apostles, and some of whom have other forms of church government. They are disturbed when they encounter Lutherans who have little interest in the question of succession of bishops, or who seem to imply that episcopacy is like a mild infection, perhaps unavoidable, but better if cleared up.

Lutherans have been equally concerned about the apostolicity of the church, but because of their experience approach the problem in a quite different way. For the Reformers bishops were not of great assistance in preserving the apostolicity of the church. Quite the contrary, in fact. There was no shortage of bishops in the 16th century, but the majority of them were quite content to let the preaching of justification by grace through faith be condemned as heresy. They assented to the expulsion of the Reformers from the church for teachings and practices which have been acclaimed by the bishops of the Second Vatican Council. In spite of this experience the Lutheran reformers did not reject the episcopal form of church government. They approved it and would have continued it in their churches had the bishops been willing to ordain pastors and bishops for them. They regarded the succession of bishops as a valuable sign of the continuity of the church. Nor did they question the validity of the bishops of their time.

What the Lutheran reformers questioned was not the title of the bishops, but the genuineness of their performance as bishops. It is the business of the bishop to preserve the truth of Jesus Christ, to care for the people

of God, to encourage sound teaching and reject false
doctrine. What is the value of episcopal succession if the
bishops fail to proclaim and defend the gospel?

Lutherans accordingly have made the test of the church's
genuineness and apostolicity, not the possession of traditional forms of ministry, but that for which the ministry
exists: the proclamation of the gospel and the administration of the sacraments. The test is a functional one:
is the gospel being proclaimed, and are the sacraments
being properly administered? If so, Christ is present, and
where Christ is, there is the church. This means that the
church is committed to do theology in a serious way, so
that it knows how to interpret the Scriptures and to discern
if Christ is being effectively proclaimed.

This test is not as easy to apply as Lutherans have sometimes assumed. There is a natural human craving for guar-
antees beyond that of God's word of promise. We Lutherans detect this tendency at work when episcopacy or
papacy is urged as an extra guarantee. We can see it
easily enough also when a pattern of piety or morality or
a certain kind of experience are used as tests of Christian
genuineness. It is more difficult for us when the inspiration of Scripture or the orthodoxy of a theological system
is put forward as the guarantee. For here we have often
misunderstood our own tradition and have been too ab-
stractly intellectual in our theology. Article VII of the
Augsburg Confession says that what is necessary to the
unity of the church is agreement in the proclamation of
the gospel and in the administration of the sacraments.
The German text of the confession makes clear that what
is meant is the actual proclamation of the gospel in preaching and in celebration of the sacraments. Lutherans have

sometimes understood this not as a functional test but as a requirement for agreement in every item in a theological system. This has led in practice to the unhappy spectacle of one school of Lutheran theologians denying the name of Lutheran to representatives of another theological emphasis. Testing the genuineness of the gospel in the church is not simply a matter of persuading other people to accept our theological formulas. For there is the prior question: how can we be sure that we are preaching the gospel? Does our theology equip us to expound the Scriptures so that we actually communicate the love of God in Jesus Christ? Or does the congregation hear one of the homiletical alternatives to the gospel: thunderbolts from Mt. Sinai, promptings to sincerity, or merely eruptions of anxiety and hostility from a frustrated pastor? Does the administration of the sacraments come through as God's offer of life in Christ or as an opportunity to pile up credit in heaven and demonstrate our earnestness, or merely as time-honored routine.

How to Keep Conversation Going

The Anglican-Lutheran conversations thus bring together representatives of churches which agree that the church is one, holy, catholic and apostolic, but differ in the way they test apostolicity. To Lutherans the Anglican pattern seems to repose too much confidence in bishops and to demand too little from the theologian. Anglicans find Lutherans overconfident and too abstract in their theology, and not sufficiently concerned with the practical working out of theology in worship and ethics. The situation offered opportunities for misunderstandings and irritations which can provide splendid raw material for the writing of comedy but can prevent serious theological encounter. For each church has in its membership and among its theologians enthusiasts for the special emphasis and excellences of its own tradition and who can stress them to the degree that they tend to exclude others. Thus there are Anglicans who can give the impression that bishops in the apostolic succession are alone a sufficient guarantee of the apostolicity of the church, and that those groups unfortunate enough to lack bishops are seriously deficient if indeed they can be spoken of as churches at all.

On the other hand there are Lutherans who give the impression that the only way to unity is the adoption, completely and without reservation, of the theological system of their party in the church. Fortunately, however, neither of these exclusivist tendencies were to hinder fruitful theological encounter between Anglicans and Lutherans in the conversations just completed. Although the discussions were explorations of somewhat unfamiliar ground to both sides, both were sufficiently resourceful to be able to adapt to the methods and outlook of the other side. The results may be important contributions to the ecumenical flexibility of both traditions.

Lutherans came to realize that not every church shares their enthusiasm for detailed and exhaustive doctrinal discussion. The production of lists of theological theses has been a standard part of the foreign policy of Lutheran synods in their relation to other synods, but impresses many churchmen today as a survival of the medieval classroom disputation rather than a means to understanding among the churches. Roman Catholic and Reformed theologians have the background and experience to take part in this type of discussion, and find in it a certain community of interest with Lutherans. But theologians of the Orthodox tradition as well as Anglicans and many representatives of the Free Churches find it foreign if not repellent. Lutherans are called upon to rediscover some neglected emphases in their own tradition in order to relate helpfully to these groups.

One such emphasis is recovered in the realization that the Reformers' program for the unity of the church, agreement on the proclamation of the gospel and the administration of the sacraments, means an assessment of the actual life of the congregations, and not merely comparison of theological formulas. Is the gospel actually being proclaimed, and are the sacraments administered so that forgiveness is actually offered to repentant sinners? In the light of what we now know of the diversity of theological styles in the New Testament church this could mean agreement on the gospel even though theological interpretations show a range of variations corresponding to those in the Scriptures. And it might mean that some searching questions need to be asked even if the same theological language is being used. This realization does not simplify the task of theology, nor in any way diminish it. It demands at the center of things a firm sense of what the gospel is, and the sensitivity to recognize it amid wide variations in vocabulary and theological style. It also requires that theology keep in touch with all of the areas and ways in which the gospel is proclaimed in the church, in worship, evangelism, mission, teaching, service, pastoral care, discipline and administration.

The exercise of this program may mean that in some cases theological discussion will not be the leading edge of the Lutheran encounter with other churches. It may mean that Lutherans adapt themselves to the other community's way of testing the genuineness of church life, and make doctrinal discussion a second phase in the relationships of the churches. This does not mean that it is less important, but that churches, like persons, must be addressed where they are and not at the point we think they should be. A consultation of Lutherans taking part in theological conversations reflected on these matters at sessions in Geneva in November 1971 and made the following recommendation:

"In particular situations *communicatio in sacris* ('communion in sacred things,' fellowship at the Lord's Supper, for example) and its acknowledgement may properly *precede* the attempt to state doctrinal consensus in the form of agreed statements. A judgment that consent in the gospel and its sacraments exists must precede *communicatio in sacris;* but this judgment may be made concrete in other ways than by explicit propositions about what the gospel is, particularly where the other communion is not accustomed so to proceed. The communions entering fellowship must simultaneously arrange to further in the future their unity in the gospel, and Lutherans will expect that these efforts will include doctrinal discussion and formulation."

This resolution will seem to many Lutherans an important departure from traditional Lutheran ways of working. The Lutherans experience of discussion with other churches has been limited until recently to encounters with Roman Catholics and Reformed churchmen, groups who operate theologically in styles quite similar to Lutheran ways. It is therefore not surprising that Lutherans have developed certain patterns of searching for doctrinal consensus. But while the resolution recommends a practice which is a change from traditional Lutheran tactics, it should not be said that it is a departure from Lutheran confessional principles, especially the classical formulation of them in the Augsburg Confession. The process will no doubt bring about some changes in the theological method of those who engage in such discussions. The necessity to view things from different perspectives need not, however, be a prelude to disaster. It can equally well bring enriched insights to Lutherans, just as conversation with Lutherans may bring enrichment to other churches. It is certainly a notable part of the ecumenical give and take that our papers are graded by others, that we confront the questions other people are asking, and that we hear, not just the echo of our own voice, but the stimulation and evaluations of others who confess Jesus Christ as Lord.

Anglicans also need to make adaptations in order to have conversations with Lutherans. Their traditional stance in the ecumenical movement has been that of the Lambeth statement which specifies four signs of the church: faith in the gospel, the authority of the Scriptures, the gospel sacraments, and episcopacy. The first three of these have been thought of as marks of catholicity and the fourth, episcopacy, has been connected with apostolicity. Anglicans recognize that in order to meet Lutherans in constructive discussion they must think of apostolicity and catholicity in relation to all four of the signs. On this basis they can acknowledge the Lutheran church as a church and postpone the question of episcopacy to a second stage of the discussions. Some Anglicans will be unhappy about this change of procedure, just as some

Lutherans will oppose making doctrinal discussion follow upon some kind of churchly recognition.

Fellowship, Cooperation, and Discussion

On the basis of this adaptation the two Anglican-Lutheran discussion groups make recommendations that are quite similar. Both propose recognition of the other as a church of Christ, continued theological discussion at the regional level of the questions which tend to be divisive, and a rather cautious movement toward more expressions of fellowship in the Lord's Supper and in various forms of cooperative work.

1. Both groups recommend intercommunion under carefully defined conditions. Communion of members of both churches at the altars of the other under emergency conditions is to be recognized as legitimate. Congregations which have come to know and trust each other are encouraged to worship together and to receive each other's members at communion. Some would call this arrangement selective fellowship: permission for individual congregations to have intercommunion although neither church has declared full fellowship with the other. The international discussion proposes specifically that the arrangements now existing for hospitality at the Eucharist between Anglicans and Swedish and Finnish Lutherans should be extended to include all European Lutheran churches.

2. Both conversations recommend that there should be continued discussion of the issues on which Anglicans and Lutherans are not in agreement, such as the nature of the gospel, forms of ministry and oversight, and sacramental

practice. Within the framework of church fellowship, each communion can continue to explore the ways in which the other witnesses to Christ and to share with the other what its own stewardship of the gospel has enabled it to see and to give. The American participants suggest in addition that each church should invite consultants from the other to take part in all deliberations dealing either with doctrinal questions or matters of sacramental practice and church order. In this way each church would consider the viewpoint of the other in dealing with questions which are important for the life of the church, insuring an ecumenical dimension to these discussions.

3. The international group made two other recommendations. Where, as in Asia and Africa, a need is felt for more rapid movement towards church union for the sake of the spread of the gospel, it should be encouraged. The recognition that both churches are apostolic and have apostolic ministries may encourage attempts at integration of ministries. Where this is done, nothing should call in question the status of existing ministries as true ministries of word and sacrament.

Where possible, cooperation should be undertaken between the churches in evangelism, social witness and in education, including programs to promote literacy, publication of Christian literature and sharing of facilities at universities and in youth centers. In areas where one of the churches may have very small congregations those of the other tradition may well offer the use of its facilities or incorporate the smaller group into its parish life, at the same time making arrangements for the group to remain in touch with its own church body.

VI

THE ROMAN CATHOLIC CHURCH: THE LORD'S SUPPER

Theological Conversations with Roman Catholics are a development of just the last decades. Previously there were cordial relationships between individual Lutherans and Roman Catholics, limited exchanges in colleges and seminaries, a few gestures by far-seeing and courageous ecumenists in both groups, but no possibility of significant relationships between churches as institutions. The Roman Catholic claims were exclusivist and seemed dogmatically final: The Roman Catholic church is the true Christian church, and the only way to Christian unity is through submitting to its claims, and returning to fellowship with the Bishop of Rome. There were, it is true, signs of renewal in the life of the Catholic church: biblical studies, the liturgical movement, the rediscovery of the theology of St. Thomas, concern for the church's impact upon the modern world, and a small handful of courageous but

beleaguered ecumenists. In those days the life of the
Catholic ecumenist was difficult. He was suspected by
many Catholics of subversive tendencies, a willingness to
make concessions to heretics and schismatics. He was suspected by Protestants of insincerity. Since the position of
the church was quite clear, the only purpose the Catholic
ecumenist could have would be to lay snares for naive
Protestants.

The Impact of Vatican II

Then came Pope John XXIII, Pope Paul VI, the Second Vatican Council and a theological upheaval un-
matched since the Reformation. Suspicious Protestants and
die-hard Catholics can still pretend that nothing has
really happened. But if this is so, it is hard to understand what the agitation in the Catholic church is really
about. The Second Vatican Council made no new dogmatic pronouncements, and changed none of the old
ones. Yet it brought about changes in the Catholic church,
in its worship, its approach to the Bible and tradition, in
its thinking about the church and its relationship to the
world, in its stand on religious freedom, in the relationship of the bishops to the pope, in the education of its
priests, in its relationship to the Jewish community, to
the world religions and to atheists, and in the way the
church is governed. Many progressives are disappointed
that the changes were not more radical, and that the pace
of carrying them out is so slow. But some conservatives
are in a state of shock that two successive Popes could
let things get so badly out of hand.

The changes affecting the relationship of the Catholic

church to other churches are numerous and far-reaching in their implications. The Catholic church for the first time in modern history has acknowledged the existence of other churches as churches. It has always recognized the existence of Christian individuals outside of its membership, in spite of what less informed Catholics or Protestant opinions have maintained. But in Vatican II it recognized that communities of Christians exist, through whom the Holy Spirit does his saving work. These churches are regarded as imperfect, for they lack communion with Rome and many have other insufficiencies as well, but they are still churches, have the Word of God, worship, faith, and bring honor to the name of Christ. This means that the Catholic church must deal with them not as a scattering of individuals, but as communities. It acknowledges that some of them, the Orthodox churches for example, and possibly Anglicans, have bishops who are to be recognized as valid bishops, and therefore also a valid Eucharist and other sacraments.

A New Approach to Unity

This means a new kind of ecumenism. The return-to-Rome program is over. If Christian unity lies in the future, it is not expected by way of surrender, but rather by way of convergence, by the gradual drawing together of the churches. This means change not only for those outside the Catholic church, but in the Catholic church as well. These changes take place in the Catholic church (as they do very often also in Protestant churches) not by revoking a doctrine, but by reinterpretation. This doctrine continues to stand, but is surrounded by new interpretative material, or by other doctrines, and thus appears in a new perspective. The process may take a long time, and no one can confidently predict the outcome, but that the process of reinterpretation is under way is clear. The doctrine of Papal Infallibility of 1870 reads like religious absolutism, and has been understood so by theologians. Vatican II places alongside it statements about the collegial relationship of the bishops to the pope and offers the possibility of a new process of development. How it comes out depends on many factors, not all of them theological, such as, for instance, the way the bishops make use of the new relationships in this generation.

Another aspect of reinterpretation may be called shift of focus. When Catholics were fighting Protestants they focussed on the doctrines that were denied by the Reformers. They asserted the institutional and legal character of the church against the Reformers' emphasis upon the freedom of the Christian, on the importance of the hierarchy against the doctrine of the priesthood of all believers. Vatican II shifts the focus to the church as God's work in history, as the people of God, as the priesthood of all believers. The shift does not produce a complete change overnight, but over a period of years should have remarkable effects upon Catholic theology, adding a push of conciliar authority and prestige to movements which already had momentum in Catholic theology. Similarly, instead of continuing to focus on the tension between Scripture and tradition, Vatican II moves attention to the historical-critical study of the Bible and suggests a different relationship between Scripture and tradition. Tradition, it suggests, consists of the ways in which the message of the Scriptures is handed on in the church.

Discussions between the churches need not now rehash all the questions at issue in the 16th century, but confront the issues raised in all the churches by the historical study of the Bible.

Discussions Begin: Dogma and Baptism

Given these changes in outlook, a new openness to other churches, and the theological momentum of Vatican II, the time seemed favorable for attempts at theological discussion between Lutherans and Catholics, and in 1965 a group of about twenty theologians met under the joint sponsorship of the American Bishops' Commission for Ecumenical Affairs and the U.S.A. Committee of the Lutheran World Federation. They set as their topic for discussion "The Status of the Nicene Creed as a Dogma of the Church." There were several reasons for choosing this topic. Both Catholics and Lutherans regard the Nicene Creed as having authority, and therefore began discussion with something held in common and not at once with disputed doctrines. The question of the creed's authority seemed to offer a good opportunity to compare ways of doing theology in the two churches. The Nicene Creed also focuses on the relationship of Jesus Christ to God, and thus introduces an issue of great importance today.

The discussion at this first meeting showed that although Catholics and Lutherans differ theologically in many ways they agree on the essential message of the Nicene Creed, on its importance in affirming that Jesus Christ is not a mere creature, but unique Son, and on the abiding authority of the creed as a doctrinal affirmation in the church. The exploration of differences in theological method, vocabulary and style was also of great value, in helping each side to understand something of the other's way of understanding the Scriptures, and the function of doctrine. It became clear that the use of the same words did not necessarily mean the same thing, and that basic agreements were sometimes phrased in quite different language. The discussions were frank and both groups were pleased at the degree of agreement which emerged during the sessions.

The second session discussed the topic "One Baptism for the remission of sins," a continuation of the discussion of the Nicene Creed in the previous meeting by narrowing in on one item in the creed. It was a continuation also in caution and prudence, taking up a topic on which there is substantial agreement among the churches. The discussions were again frank and cordial, revealing substantial areas of agreement in the understanding of the Scriptures, of the function of sacraments in the church and on the meaning and importance of baptism. One area of difference which emerged, and which continued during the following meetings to call for the attention of the group, was the question of the minister of the sacrament. This indication that the doctrine of the ministry was involved also in questions about the sacraments came as a surprise to no one, and influenced the groups to turn to questions of ministry sooner than they might otherwise have done.

Eucharist as Sacrifice

The discussions on baptism were sufficiently satisfying to encourage the group to undertake more controversial topics. It was decided to turn to a discussion of "Eucharist as Sacrifice," a topic on which very harsh words have been spoken by both sides. The doctrinal lines between the churches have been clearly drawn, and the disagreements so deep and so vehemently stated as to appear beyond possibility of reconciliation.

Catholics have interpreted the Mass or the Lord's Supper as a sacrifice, and not simply as a sacrifice of praise and thanksgiving as the Reformers were quite willing to grant. It is an unbloody sacrifice, a repetition of Calvary offered by the priest on behalf of the people, and has atoning or propitiatory effect, that is, it brings about a change in the relationships between God and man, enabling God to forgive sin and receive the sinner into his presence.

The Reformers rejected this. They argued that the death of Christ on the Cross was a once-for-all act of self-offering which accomplished atonement or propitiation for the sins of mankind. To speak of the Mass as a sacrifice in this sense raises questions about the sufficiency of Christ's death, and strikes at the heart of the Christian's assurance of forgiveness and salvation.

They insisted further that the sacrifice of Christ is a movement from God to man, and not from man to God. The heart of the gospel is its announcement that salvation is the work of God; it does not depend upon human worthiness or works. To suggest that men offer something to God is to introduce the matter of human accomplishments into a place where it does not belong. It also introduces confusion at a point where clarity is especially important. To be sure of his own salvation man must be

clear that his hope of life rests not on his own performance but solely on the work and promise of God in Christ.

Catholics have heard the Reformers' objections with
dismay. They have seen in them a denial of the Lord's
Supper as a sacrament, a denial that the benefits of the
Cross are imparted to worshippers, a denial of Christ's
presence in the Supper, and of the unity creating power
of the sacrament, and therefore a threat to substitute individual piety for the fellowship of the community.

The intensity of the controversy has given the impression that Catholics and Lutherans have no common
ground, but stand on opposite sides of an unbridgeable
chasm. Controversy often has this effect, so that it is
useful to try to locate elements which are common to the
parties in the argument.

Both churches agree that the Mass or Lord's Supper is
a liturgical act of central importance in the life of the
people of God. They agree that there is a connection with
Calvary; that somehow the benefits of Calvary are given
to believers as they take part in the Supper. They agree
that the word sacrifice has been used in connection with
the Supper and that this use is appropriate, although they
diverge sharply on how the word should be interpreted.
Thus it is not as simple a divergence as between those
who affirm faith in God and those who deny it. Both sides
bring to the discussion convictions about the work of
God among men, about the meaning and effect of the
death of Christ and about the sacrament as a channel of
God's blessing to his people. The common elements are
present, if only they are noticed, and what is held in
common outweighs the differences, although it has been
hard to see this until the contribution of biblical studies

and comparative religion transformed the discussion of this topic.

The New Understanding of Sacrifice

Biblical studies, especially the work of men like Bishop F. C. N. Hicks in *The Fullness of Sacrifice,* have led to major changes in the understanding of the work of Christ and the meaning of the Lord's Supper. Interpreting Christ's work as sacrifice has caused difficulties for theologians for centuries. They seemed to have lost an understanding or feeling for what sacrifice is in the realm of religion, and had sounded like tone deaf men writing music criticism. Anselm offered an interpretation of sacrifice for the men of his time that made use of ideas of the honor of God, and the satisfaction due to his honor, ideas common in feudalism and the code of chivalry. He interpreted the death of Christ as supplying the satisfaction due to God's honor on behalf of men, who because of their sin and guilt were unable to satisfy it. John Calvin later offered another set of pictures, building upon the image of the wrath and judgment of God upon sin. Christ stands in man's place before the righteous judgment of God, and endures the punishment which is due to men. Thus the cost of human sin has been paid, and men can through faith in Christ enter the presence of God not as enemies but as Sons.

The rediscovery of the meaning of ritual worship through studies in the Bible and comparative religion gives a new setting to the term. Sacrifice is not a system of barter in which men offer gifts to God in the hope that his anger will be appeased and he will look upon them with favor. God neither needs men's gifts nor is he susceptible to bribes. He loves his creatures in spite of their disobedience, and moves out in persuasive love to win them back to himself. His justice or wrath stands in the way of man's restoration, not in the sense that God's feelings have been hurt and his injured vanity is in need of appeasement, but because the world has been made with a certain structure. Man has been made for fellowship and harmony with God, and can develop his possibilities as a human being only in this relationship. Man should worship God with his whole being not because God's self esteem needs man's tributes, but because worship of God is an essential condition of humanity. Sin is man's choice of himself and his own autonomy rather than the context of life in God. And the judgment of sin is not God striking the evil doer in petulant fury, but man's discovery, the hard way, that his life just doesn't function properly when it is lived egocentrically.

The ritual of sacrifice is a device by which man can recover his true humanity. In it he goes to school to learn that he lives by God's goodness, and only in acknowledging God's kingship in the act of giving himself wholly to God does he begin to recover his true creaturehood, his genuine humanity. The meaning of sacrifice is thus not to buy God's favor, but to offer one's self to God by identification with the offering which is placed on the altar. Each step in the ritual procedure is meaningful. Man approaches the altar, and in doing so draws near to God. He places his hands upon the gift which he is giving, not to transfer his sins, but to identify himself with it. (In Old Testament religion sins are indeed transferred to a scapegoat, but the goat is not sacrificed, but driven away into the wilderness, Lev. 16:20-22). Then the animal is killed, not as punishment for the sins which he now carries but so that his blood, which to Old Testament religion is the life, may be offered before God by sprinkling on the altar. Next a portion of the offering is burned, as a sign of its dedication to God, and finally another portion of the offering is eaten by the worshipper and the priest, as the sharing of meal fellowship with God. The inner meaning of the sacrificial ritual is therefore the sacrificer's offering of himself to God and God's gracious acceptance of him.

The New Testament interprets the sacrificial system of the Old Covenant as a provisional, preparatory ritual. It can be misunderstood quite easily, in spite of the prophet's attempts to interpret it, because it is incomplete. Only with the coming of Christ does it become apparent what the ritual really signifies. Sacrifice is not a movement from man to God, but from God to man. Man the sinner does not succeed in worshipping in spirit and in truth. He offers his gift, but withholds himself, and thus performs a deceitful gesture. He tries to fool God with a lie. Only in Christ is sacrifice offered in reality and truth. His entire life is an obedient offering of himself and all that he is to God, climaxing in his self-offering on Calvary. What could be seen as the attempt of men to gain favor with God now appears in a different light. It is the ritual which God makes available to man, so that he may make the self-offering which fulfils his humanity. No worshipper under the Old Covenant or today approaches God without reserving some things for himself. Thus our worship is falsified. Only by our union with Christ are we able to participate in a complete self-giving to God, and thus begin in Christ to be genuine human beings.

Given this understanding of sacrifice, the religious concerns of both churches can be satisfied without the necessity of using language which offends the other group. Lutherans find a clear statement that sacrifice is a movement from God to man, and that man's part in the Supper is his response in faith to God's word of promise. The language of an unbloody repetition of Calvary is no longer used, and the once-for-all character of Christ's death is firmly stated. Catholics hear Lutherans affirm the close connection between Calvary and the Supper and the gift of the benefits of Christ's death to those who take part in faith. And both see the image of sacrifice set in the midst of a rich and diverse interpretation of the meaning of Christ's mission and death and of the significance of the coming of the risen Christ to fellowship with his people in the sacrament.

The Presence of Christ

A discussion of the Lord's Supper between Catholics and Lutherans inevitably involves also the question of the real presence of Christ. The Catholic doctrine of transubstantiation has been a point of especially heated controversy and of vigorous denunciations on both sides.

Lutherans have understood the doctrine of transubstantiation to mean four things.

1. An emphatic statement of the presence of Christ in the Supper. To this they have no objection. Luther, in fact, suggests that if compelled to choose between a Zwin-

glian understanding of the Supper and transubstantiation he would unhesitatingly choose the latter. His reason was that whatever objections he had to it, the doctrine of transubstantiation firmly asserts the presence of Christ while the Zwinglian approach makes it very questionable.

2. An assertion that God acts in the Lord's Supper, changing bread and wine into the body and blood of Christ. Lutherans can also affirm this and the Lutheran confessions do so, but are reluctant to use the word change or transformation, because of fears that transformation of elements will be understood as the annihilation of the elements. Lutherans have preferred to speak of the bread and wine remaining bread and wine, and yet becoming the means in the sacramental meal of the presence of the risen and regnant Christ.

3. An explanation of the way bread and wine become the body and blood of Christ. Catholic theologians have used philosophical language to state that the "attributes" remain those of bread and wine (color, texture, taste, etc.), but that the "substance" becomes the body and blood of Christ. Lutherans believe that Jesus Christ is present because of his word of promise, and regard any explanation of how he is present as completely beyond human understanding. Explanations of this kind are therefore at best a waste of effort, and at worst an exercise in irreverence.

4. An insistence that the philosophical-theological language of the Middle Ages is the only language which can be used to define the meaning of the Lord's Supper. In view of the plurality of theologies in the Bible and the

variety of theological languages available today, this seems unnecessarily narrow and limiting.

Catholics have had strenuous objections to Lutheran teaching also. To them the rejection of the doctrine of transubstantiation has sounded like a denial of the real presence. That Lutheran pastors have not been ordained by bishops in the apostolic succession has seemed like a carelessness about the validity and effectiveness of the Lord's Supper in Lutheran churches. They have therefore lumped Lutherans together with other Protestants as rebels who have made such devastating changes in the church that hardly anything of Christian substance is left: bishops, ministry, sacraments, church and mission seem all to have eroded away and left nothing more than religious phrases and good intentions. Baptism in the name of the Triune God remains an isolated rock left after a destructive flood. Individual Christians there may be, but the poverty of their nourishment and the absence of the fellowship of the people of God leave them scant hope of growth to healthy life.

The discussions on this topic were illuminating to both sides. Catholics became aware of the Lutheran concern for loyalty to the Scriptures and creeds, for continuing in the apostolic gospel, for the proper administration of the sacraments, for a ministry which serves Christ and his people, for the real presence in the Supper. As a result they find themselves called to rethink many of their traditional judgments on the theology and church life of Lutherans, considerations which are of importance also for the discussion of the ministry in the Church.

Lutherans observe the impact of renewal movements and of Vatican II in the theological thought and congregational life of Catholics and come to a new understanding of the Catholic position. They are assured that the dogma of transubstantiation intends to affirm the presence of Christ and of the change in the elements of bread and wine in the sacrament, and that it is not an attempt to explain how Christ is present. On these terms Lutherans can acknowledge that it is a legitimate way to express the mystery of the presence, although they themselves regard the word transubstantiation as one which creates much misunderstanding, and therefore prefer not to use it in their own discussions.

The question of theological language is much discussed in modern Catholic theology. There are theologians for whom the traditional language is the only satisfactory way to discuss theological questions. There are also many theologians, including the most influential ones today, who agree with the Lutheran-Catholic statement that "no single vocabulary or conceptual framework can be adequate, exclusive or final in this theological enterprise. We are convinced that current theological trends in both traditions give great promise for increasing convergence and deepened understanding of the eucharistic mystery."

Convergence in Worship

One additional aspect of this matter needs to be noted. Theological developments in both churches lead not only to convergence in understanding of doctrine but convergence also in the life of worship, witness and service. The revisions in the Mass in the Catholic church have been far-reaching and have resulted in a service which in many countries is hard to distinguish from the service in a

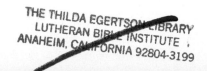

Lutheran church. The liturgical forms are strikingly similar, Scripture readings and hymns increasingly alike, the arrangements within the church buildings more and more resemble each other. The increased participation of the congregation in the Catholic liturgy and the greater emphasis upon the reading and exposition of the Word of God also contribute to a growing sense of convergence.

The participants in the Catholic-Lutheran conversations do not claim to have resolved all of the differences on the theology and practice of the two churches. They are careful to note the areas which have not been discussed, or not discussed sufficiently, and specify areas where more discussion is necessary. What is important is that the issues which have been so divisive in the past have been discussed thoroughly enough to be sure that there is solid agreement. This is in large part due to previous work done under the auspices of Faith and Order at Edinburgh in 1937. Here the foundations were laid on which even wider agreements are now possible between Anglicans and Catholics, and Reformed and Catholics. It is a great gift of the Spirit to the churches that the disagreements of the past are being overcome and that Christians of many different traditions can agree on the meaning of the Lord's Supper and on the blessings which God bestows upon his people through Christ's presence in their midst. That the Sacrament of the Altar is once again becoming the sacrament of unity in the church is occasion for thanksgiving.

VII

THE ROMAN CATHOLIC CHURCH: THE MINISTRY

At the beginning of the discussion of the Lord's Supper many of those taking part in the Catholic-Lutheran conversations had confidence that the traditional differences could be overcome. The question had received considerable attention in ecumenical discussion and notable progress had already been made. No one could have the same confidence in approaching the discussion of the ministry. This topic too had received much attention in ecumenical discussion, and many caricatures and misunderstandings had been put aside, but the positions of the churches remained unchanged. Those who had bishops in the apostolic succession were reluctant to have full fellowship with churches which had other forms of government. The churches not having bishops in the apostolic succession did not consider themselves less apostolic or catholic because of this lack, and were unwilling to consider plans for unity which suggested that their shortcomings must be attended to before fellowship was possible.

Can This Chasm Be Bridged?

The discussions began with the daunting prospect of an unscalable and impenetrable wall of division. In such discussions Lutherans have at least the small advantage that though they do not regard bishops in apostolic succession as essential to the church, some Lutheran churches have such bishops and the others are opposed to them only if they are made a requirement. Lutherans are quite willing to recognize as churches those that claim apostolic succession, even if they do not extend the same recognition to Lutherans. To Lutherans their defect is not lack of apostolicity (which must be tested on grounds other than the mere possession of episcopacy) but a certain rigidity on questions of theology and church law.

Since the Reformation the Lutherans have held that it is enough for the true unity of the church that there be agreement in the proclamation of the gospel and in the administration of the sacraments. In all other matters a wide diversity of positions and practices is possible. Churches may have any form of administration which serves the effective proclamation of the gospel. Wide variations in liturgy are possible, although not such as deny the gospel or distort the sacraments. There are many options on church discipline, on relations to the state, in patterns of piety, ethics, and missionary methods.

As noted in Chapter 5 the meaning of this position has often been misunderstood in Lutheran circles. Some have supposed that agreement in the proclamation of the gospel means point by point agreement on every item in a Lutheran theological system, a procedure difficult enough within the Lutheran family and quite visionary with respect to most other churches. What it means is the application of such tests as will enable the churches to recognize that the gospel is indeed being proclaimed and that the sacraments are being administered properly. It is not necessary that human traditions, including theology as well as church government, be everywhere the same.

The test of the living proclamation of the gospel is a complex one, not to be settled simply by examination of the church's creeds and confessions or its manuals of theology. It requires attention to the worship of the congregations, the preaching of its pastors, the patterns of administering the sacraments, instruction in the Christian faith at every level, the congregation's outreach in service to the community, its missionary program, its concern for those who are generally neglected, such as the poor, the old and victims of discrimination. No church today emerges from this examination with honors, but in the process churches can detect in each other the authentic presence of Jesus Christ and the gifts of the Holy Spirit. The Lutheran reformers asked no more than this.

For the Catholic church the chief sign of unity is fellowship with the Bishop of Rome, whose task it is as successor of Peter to preserve the unity of the church in Catholic doctrine, worship and discipline. Formerly Catholic theologians identified the institutional Roman Catholic church as the true church of Christ and acknowledged the existence of only individual Christians outside its fellowship. At Vatican II, however, it recognized that the church of Jesus Christ is the people of God, the mystery of God at work in the world and stated that this church *subsists* chiefly in the Roman Catholic church. It also recognized that there are other churches, having valid ministries and true sacraments, although they are partly defective because they are not in communion with the Bishop of Rome. It is on the basis of this changed viewpoint that discussions with Catholic theologians hold new promise.

Surprising Agreements on the Ministry

The discussions on the ministry occupied four sessions of three full days each, together with several meetings of sub-committees for drafting and editing. They resulted in a statement of agreements which may be as significant for the relationships between the two churches as the earlier agreement on the Lord's Supper. Each of the previous discussions, on the Nicene Creed, on Baptism, on the Eucharist and on Intercommunion had shown that there were problems in each area which could be adequately discussed only if attention were given to the problem of the ministry.

Throughout the discussions attempts were made to keep the Catholic-Lutheran conversations in close relationship to the discussion of these problems in Faith and Order, especially to the 1963 Conference on Faith and Order held in Montreal. The findings of the group at Montreal working on problems of the ministry raise basic questions about the relationship of ordained ministers to the ministry of the whole people of God, about ordination as a commitment to a lifetime of service, and about the necessity and viability of traditional structures of the ministry in the third world, particularly in Africa with its many new religious movements. There are many dangers to the younger churches in the tendency of the denominations to export their divisions and theological tensions along with the gospel. The ecumenical movement has been made well aware of these dangers, and the Catholic-Lutheran discussions attempted to maintain them on their horizon.

The statement of agreements observes that "neither Catholic nor Lutheran participants came to this dialogue with a complete doctrine of the Ministry, and we have not formulated one in our discussions." "We have found certain areas that we judge are central to this reality and critical for the unity of the church. In these areas we make common affirmations."

1. Both churches see the Ministry in the context of God's work of salvation in Christ. God has made promises to his covenant people which he fulfills in the life and ministry of Jesus Christ, thus revealing his saving love. He has sent his Holy Spirit to call men to repentance, to announce to them the good news, and to bind them together in Christ in the fellowship of the Christian community. He continues to act for the salvation of the world through the proclamation of the gospel and the administration of the sacraments in the church. The church, the people of God, has the continuing task of proclaiming the gospel to all men, believers and unbelievers alike. This task is spoken of as the "ministry" of the church. Within the ministry or service of the church there is a special Ministry (distinguished from the ministry of all believers by the use of the capital M), whose task it is to equip and enable the people of God for their service in and for the world.

2. Both groups also agree that this special Ministry in

the church cannot be discussed except in the context of the ministry of the whole church. All believers are called in their baptism to be a holy priesthood in Christ, and to share in his ongoing priestly work of representing God to men and interceding with God for men. The New Testament sees this priesthood of all believers supported and served by a variety of ministries or services; apostles, prophets, teachers, evangelists, pastors, healing, administration. "While no single ministry mentioned in the New Testament corresponds exactly to the special Ministry of the later church, many of the specialized tasks of which we hear in the New Testament are entrusted to that later Ministry: preaching the gospel, administering what the church came to call sacraments, caring for the faithful."

3. Both the church and the Ministry are to be seen in the light of the love of God, his saving act in Jesus Christ and the ongoing activity of the Holy Spirit. The Ministry has a two-fold task: proclaiming the gospel to the world in witness and service, and building up in Christ those who already have faith, teaching, exhorting, reproving and sanctifying through word and sacrament. The Ministry exists for the sake of the people and their service in the world. In order that the Ministry may help the church meet new situations in its pilgrimage, the Spirit sends a variety of gifts for its equipment, growth and maintenance of unity.

4. The Ministry belongs to the people of God, and stands with them under the judgment and grace of God. Ministers too are sinners and need forgiveness and the support of their fellow Christians. On the other hand, the Ministry has a special role within the ministry of the

whole people, proclaiming the Word of God, administering the sacraments, exhorting and reproving.

5. Both groups agree that the Ministry is apostolic and that the word apostolic means several different things. In the early church succession in the doctrine of the gospel was a sign of apostolicity. Under the pressures of doctrinal distortion and persecution an emphasis on succession in apostolic office developed as a way of ensuring the doctrinal succession and providing both a sign of unity and a defense of sound doctrine. Lutherans have understood apostolic succession as continuity in the doctrine of the gospel. Catholics have understood it as succession in ministerial office as a sign of unbroken transmission from the apostles. In their modern theological development both churches have realized that apostolic succession is maintained in a diversity of ways: the liturgy, creeds and confessions, administration of the sacraments, preaching and teaching, evangelism, missions, pastoral care, church discipline, the services of elders, deacons, pastors, bishops. None of these in isolation is an adequate sign of continuity, but all together they give assurance that the church is indeed the apostolic church, the people sent into the world by Jesus Christ.

6. There is substantial agreement on the meaning of ordination. Catholics see it as a sacramental act, involving a gift of the Holy Spirit, appointment to the service of the church and the world, and a quality of permanence and unrepeatability. Lutherans have been reluctant to call ordination a sacrament, although one of the Lutheran confessions, the Apology of the Augsburg Confession, does so. This reluctance is partly derived from a more

restricted definition of sacrament than that used by Catholics, partly due to post-Reformation polemics about ordination and the sacraments in general.

But when Catholics hear Lutherans explain the practice of their church in ordination, they detect a conviction concerning what they call the sacramental reality of ordination. Lutherans too invoke the Holy Spirit for the gifts of the Ministry, see ordination as a setting apart for a specific service in the church and for the world and regard it as an act which is not to be repeated. At the level of practice of ordination therefore, if not of theological terminology, there is a growing convergence between the two churches.

7. The words "indelible character" have in the past been the subject of controversy. Catholics have used them in connection with ordination as a way of describing the aspects of the Spirit's gift, designation for a special service and the permanence of the calling. Lutherans have objected to them because of the metaphysical implications they understood as involved in them. They see the ordained person as set apart for a special task and in need of special gifts from the Spirit such as wisdom, endurance and insight, but not as differing from the unordained Christian by virtue of some special or supernatural quality. Historical studies have shown that the original meaning of indelible character did not have such metaphysical implications, and that therefore the theological intentions of Catholics and Lutherans are closer together at this point than was realized previously.

8. Catholic and Lutheran ministries are structured in different ways. In the Catholic church the Ministry is

divided into three orders, deacons, priests and bishops. All three orders are conferred by a rite of ordination that includes the laying-on of hands. The distribution of ministerial functions among these orders has varied in the past, but at present all three are appointed to baptize and proclaim the gospel, only bishops and priests preside at the Eucharist, and only bishops ordain to major orders.

The Lutheran confessions indicate that the Reformers would have preferred to maintain the traditional episcopal structure of the church together with its discipline. They were unable to do so, however, because bishops in the historical succession refused to ordain pastors for the congregations of the Reformation churches. As a result, most Lutheran churches have one order, that of pastors or presbyters, set apart by a rite of ordination by the laying-on of hands of other presbyters. The pastor in the Lutheran tradition corresponds to the bishop in the Catholic church. Lutheran bishops or church presidents are pastors elected for supervision of congregations and pastors. Ordination is usually reserved to them or to the pastor appointed by them.

The Catholic members of the group have noted that there are cases in the history of the Catholic church where priests have been ordained by priests, and regard this as both historically and theologically significant for the discussion of this question of ministry. It suggests that the Lutheran pattern of Ministry may be in accord with practices within the Catholic church as well as with the understanding of Ministry in the Scriptures and the early church. Both groups agree that the basic reality of the apostolic ministry may be preserved among variations in structures, in rites of ordination and theological explanation, and join in urging both the renewal of what is basic in the theological heritage in both churches as well as openness to the variants needed by the church in her witness to the world today.

These agreements are of considerable weight and show how the common study of the Scriptures, attention to the history of the church and its theology, and the discussions of the ecumenical movement enable churches with little theological contact in the past to move to greater understanding and to overcome differences. Perhaps of even greater importance, however, at least in their impact upon the mood of the relationships between the churches are the attached statements of each group of participants addressed to their own church.

An Important Recommendation

Lutherans review how they have seen signs of the church in the Roman Catholic community even in times of most intense theological conflict. They note the way the Reformers called attention to evangelical elements in the church of the Middle Ages, especially in the witness of men such as Bernard of Clairvaux, Francis of Assisi, Dominic, and Gerson. They call attention to many important things held in common by the two churches: confession of the great creeds, the lectionary with its Scripture lessons, the prayers of the church year, Baptism and Communion. The Reformers never rejected the episcopal structure of the Catholic church, but expressed their preference for maintaining it and the discipline that goes with it and their regret that they were not able to do so. In spite of harsh words on the subject of papacy, the Reformers did not deny that the pope is the lawful bishop of the church in Rome, nor even exclude the possibility that the papacy might have a wider ecumenical function as long as his claims are not urged as a matter of divine right. Even though they objected to the withholding of the cup from the laity at Communion, the Reformers did not deny that Catholics receive Christ in the Mass.

They call attention to the many developments in modern Roman Catholicism, especially since Vatican II, which Lutherans see as clarifying the witness to Jesus Christ and correcting practices which they have regarded as ambiguous or likely to cause misunderstanding. Among them are the emphasis upon the community's participation in the Eucharist, upon the reading of Scripture and preaching, the increasing opportunities for reception of the sacrament in both kinds, and clarification of the meaning of the Eucharist as sacrifice and of the doctrine of transubstantiation.

They acknowledge that they have not discussed all the problems that create obstacles between Catholics and Lutherans, and that the common statement does not provide an adequate basis for the establishment of pulpit and altar fellowship. Neither does it indicate approval by either community of every practice fostered or tolerated by the other community.

The concluding two paragraphs deserve to be quoted in full: "We Lutherans are conscious of the real and imagined differences that centuries of mutual separation have built up between us and Roman Catholics. We are sensitive to the canonical, traditional and psychological barriers to eucharistic sharing that are present in both communities. We are aware of the many doctrinal discussions that both the Roman Catholic and the Lutheran churches in the United States are conducting, and recognize the magnitude of the theological work that still needs to be done.

"As Lutherans, we joyfully witness that in our theological dialogue with our Roman Catholic partners we have again seen clearly a fidelity to the proclamation of the gospel and the administration of the sacraments which confirms our historic conviction that the Roman Catholic church is an authentic church of our Lord Jesus Christ. For this reason we recommend to those who have appointed us that through appropriate channels the participating Lutheran churches be urged to declare formally their judgment that the ordained Ministers of the Roman Catholic church are engaged in a valid ministry of the gospel, announcing the gospel of Christ and administering the sacraments of faith as their chief responsibilities, and that the body and blood of our Lord Jesus Christ are truly present in their celebrations of the sacrament of the altar."

The reflections of the Roman Catholic participants are more momentous both theologically and ecumenically than the statement of agreements or the reflections of the Lutherans. The agreements state what theologians of both traditions, striving to be faithful to the theological standards of their own churches, can say together today. The Lutherans recommend to their churches a statement notable mainly for the positive appreciation of the renewal taking place in contemporary Roman Catholicism and its joyful acknowledgement of the faithfulness of Roman Catholics today in proclaiming the gospel and administering the sacraments. The Roman Catholic reflections ask the authorities of the Catholic church to take an action which is theologically and ecumenically without precedent. Even if it produces no response whatever from the authorities, it is an event of importance in the relationships between the churches and cannot but have considerable impact upon the way theological work is done in the future in both churches as well as upon the atmosphere of future encounters between members of the churches.

The Catholic members recommend:

"As Roman Catholic theologians, we acknowledge in the spirit of Vatican II that the Lutheran communities with which we have been in dialogue are truly Christian churches, possessing the elements of holiness and truth that mark them as organs of grace and salvation. Furthermore, in our study we have found serious defects in the arguments customarily used against the validity of the eucharistic ministry of the Lutheran churches. In fact we see no persuasive reason to deny the possibility of the Roman Catholic church recognizing the validity of this Ministry. Accordingly we ask the authorities of the Roman Catholic church whether the ecumenical urgency flowing from Christ's will for unity may not dictate that the Roman Catholic church recognize the validity of the Lutheran Ministry and, correspondingly, the presence of the body and blood of Christ in the eucharistic celebrations of the Lutheran churches."

They prepare the way for this statement by historical and theological arguments. The historical arguments set out to show that the New Testament and patristic evidence does not clearly show that the only valid minister of the Eucharist is one ordained by a bishop, and that even in the Middle Ages when this practice was general there are some cases of priests being ordained by priests and of the church accepting their ministry as valid. Thus there is historical precedent for the pattern of ordination practiced by Lutherans.

The theological section argues that whatever the situation in the 16th century and however correct the Council of Trent in its rejection of the ministry of the Reformers at the time, the situation today is different. The Catholic church has at Vatican II acknowledged the existence of "churches or ecclesiastical communities" outside of its fellowship, and "that many of them ... celebrate the Eucharist." Moreover a more detailed acquaintance with the Lutheran churches shows that even without episcopal succession, they have preserved through their devotion to gospel, creed and sacrament a form of apostolicity. Their eucharistic teaching and practice emphasize the aspects which Catholics consider essential. Their theology and practice of ordination correspond in many ways to that of the Catholic church, in stressing its divine origin, its obligation to preach the gospel and administer the sacraments, its distinctive function in relation to the ministry of the whole people of God, and in features which Catholics describe as sacramental: the laying-on of hands, prayer for the gifts of the Spirit, designation to a special task in the church, and the unrepeatable character of the rite. Thus both a new openness to other churches on the part of the Catholic church, and a new evaluation of the doctrine and practice of the Lutheran churches suggest the possibility of a new estimation of Lutheran church structures and sacraments today.

Do Theologians Speak for the Churches?

It is important to note that however important this recommendation is in itself, there is no guarantee that the authorities of the Catholic church will respond to it favorably in the immediate or more remote future. There are Catholic bishops and theologians for whom the re-establishment of fellowship with the Orthodox churches is far higher in priority than is fellowship with the churches of the Reformation. An action such as that recommended by the American Catholic theologians would without doubt be received badly in Orthodox circles and thus complicate the search for unity with them. Moreover, sociologists have made us aware of the tendency of those in positions of authority in organizations, whether governmental, commercial, educational or ecclesiastical, to resist change, especially when it is suggested by outsiders or those in lower echelons. Simply as a matter of institutional inertia, therefore, the possibilities of an early and favorable response are not great.

There are of course factors working in favor of acceptance of the recommendation. An increasing number of Catholic theologians are in accord with the methods of theological work which underlie the Catholic-Lutheran agreement, building upon the results of historical study of the Bible and the theology of the church, attempting to do their work not in isolation but in relation to theologians of all churches, and seeking convergence on the main issues in doctrine. Many bishops in the Catholic church, including the American church, are committed to responsible ecumenical work as a part of the mission of the church today, and support such joint theological studies.

VIII

WHAT NEXT?

What do we look forward to in this development of new relationships? What do they mean for Lutheran churches, for the life of the congregation and the lives of ordinary people?

1. It is likely that the majority of Reformed and Lutheran churches will declare fellowship with each other, either on the basis of the Leuenberg Agreement or through regional conversations. Both churches will be more open to the influence of the other in theology, in patterns of worship, service and piety. This may result in an increased impact of the tradition of the Reformation in relationships among the churches. To some people it will mean new and different influences in a world which is already well equipped with irritations and stimulants. It should increase the amount of imagination applied to the problem of being the church in the modern world. It may also make the gospel of Jesus Christ somewhat more credible to men of today.

119

2. It is possible that Anglicans and Lutherans will begin to share with each other in worship and in some cooperative projects in theology, education, and evangelism. The effect of these encounters will probably be much greater in Asia and Africa than in America. Lutherans will again be confronted by different patterns of piety and different forms of church organization. In theology the question of episcopacy will certainly move forward on the agenda, for even if Roman Catholics can accept Lutherans without bishops, it is doubtful that Episcopalians can.

3. Our relationships with Roman Catholics have become more cordial, not least because of the graciousness and energy which Catholics have brought to this task. Most of the issues debated at the time of the Reformation seem to cause less argument today. Justification by grace through faith is accepted by both groups; so is the priesthood of all believers, although both churches have the task of working out the relationships between the special Ministry and the ministry of the whole people of God. The churches are drawing closer together on such questions as the authority of the Bible and its use in the church, the role of tradition, the relationship of the church to the world and many others.

Even the question of Mary and her place in the church is less troublesome than it was. The decision of Vatican II not to issue a separate theological pronouncement on Mary, but to include it as a chapter in the constitution on the church, seems to have changed the atmosphere of Catholic thinking about Mary. Even those who see themselves as having a special vocation to speak of Mary's place in the church now try to do their work in an ecumenical setting. The temperature of devotion to Mary seems to have moderated. No doubt the revisions in the Mass have had some influence at this point. The stress upon the congregation's participation in worship, and upon the role of the Scriptures and preaching have moved toward a more community-oriented and Christ-centered piety.

The problem of the papacy remains perhaps the most difficult one, both theologically and psychologically. So much harsh language has been exchanged on this issue, and so many emotions aroused, that it will be difficult to deal with the question dispassionately for some time. Theological discussions have shown that where emotional elements can be put aside the churches are not as far apart as traditional polemics would seem to indicate, although the remaining differences are indeed formidable.

Lutherans can grant, for example, that the church needs some agency for maintaining and furthering unity. This is the function which the Lutheran confessions have served since the Reformation. The confessions, however, are limited in their usefulness at this point because Lutherans themselves sometimes differ on the interpretation of them, and have no generally accepted referee to rule on disputed questions. A more serious limitation, of course, is that the confessions have little attraction for other churches. The Bishop of Rome remains the uniting factor with the longest history of usefulness in this function and with credentials which appeal to many different churches. The papacy has also accumulated many liabilities since the Middle Ages. Most people outside of the Roman

Catholic church find it too imperial both in its ceremonial and in its way of asserting power. But even papal and curial ways of governing the church may be easier to deal with than the dogmatic definition of papal primacy and authority of Vatican I.

There are many Roman Catholics who would like to see changes in the papacy in order to present to the world the figure of the Bishop of Rome as the servant of the churches. Pope Paul himself seems to share this viewpoint, and has made many changes both in the ceremonial which surrounds him and in the patterns of exercising authority in Rome. The move toward a simpler style of life and a much broader sharing of power in the church has taken place very gradually and quietly. There have been many changes, each of them perhaps of little moment by itself, and yet together they signal a perceptible shift. They may, in the long run, be just as important as the more dramatic change of style introduced by Pope John XXIII, because they seek to give organizational expression to his pastoral conception of the papal office.

There are Roman Catholics who desire changes in the theological interpretation of the papacy as well. They accept the authority of the 1870 definition of papal primacy, and seek to understand it in its historical situation. They look forward to new developments through the exercise of collegial authority on the part of the bishops, through the contributions of the Synod of Bishops and through increased delegation of power to regional and national conferences of bishops. It may be that the increasing influence of priests, nuns and lay people may also have a role in this process of development. The process will certainly be a long one, but it is to be hoped that it will take place in the context of the search for Christian unity by all the churches.

The contributions of the various theological discussions between the churches can be very important in the development of new methods and perspectives in theology. Even if their recommendations are not accepted at once, they have their effect on the atmosphere of the discussion and upon the theological priorities in the churches as well as on the kind of decision that becomes possible. If the discussions between the churches remain congenial and effective, no church can go back to doing theology in isolation or defensiveness. The whole people of God must be the horizon for all future theological work.

4. Lutherans have hardly begun to discuss theology with Orthodox churches. Neither church knows much of the worship, theology or piety of the other. Because differing attitudes toward the ecumenical movement and different strategies toward the Roman Catholic church, Orthodox churches have not been able to invest their theological energies in discussion with the churches of the Reformation. International conversations sponsored by the Orthodox Patriarchate and the Lutheran World Federation are about to begin. We may hope that they will be as successful as the other theological discussions have been in improving communications between the churches.

5. The Evian Assembly of 1970 asked the Lutheran World Federation to enter into theological conversations with Methodists, Baptists, Pentecostals and Independent Christian groups. Discussions with Methodists should not be difficult to arrange unless they regard themselves as over-extended in interconfessional theological conversa-

tions. It is more difficult with the other groups because of their stress upon the independence of the congregations and the resultant lack of international agencies to share sponsorship of such discussions.

There are many people today who would like to bypass both theology and the institutional churches in their search for unity in Christ. Their distrust of theologians and organizations is quite understandable, but their vision of an end-run around them is unrealistic. Whatever changes take place in the churches in the next decade, they will continue to have organizational structures. And although there are many differences between the churches, cultural, psychological, and theological, the theological differences are the most important and perhaps also most difficult. That the most difficult differences are now being overcome through increase of knowledge and a new process of discussion is one of the most hopeful events in our world today.

BIBLIOGRAPHY

The Nature of the Unity We Seek. Edited by Paul Minear. Bethany Press, St. Louis, Mo., 1958.

Marburg Revisited, A Reexamination of Lutheran and Reformed Traditions. Edited by Paul C. Empie and James I. McCord. Augsburg Publishing House, Minneapolis, 1966.

Lutherans and Catholics in Dialogue: The Status of The Nicene Creed as Dogma of the Church. Published Jointly by Representatives of the U.S.A. Committee of the Lutheran World Federation and the Bishops' Commission for Ecumenical Affairs, 1965.

Lutherans and Catholics in Dialogue II: One Baptism for the Remission of Sins. Edited by Paul C. Empie and William W. Baum. Published Jointly by Representatives of the U.S.A. Committee of the Lutheran World Federation and the Bishops' Commission for Ecumenical Affairs, 1966.

Lutherans and Catholics in Dialogue III: The Eucharist as Sacrifice. Published Jointly by Representatives of the U.S.A. Committee of the Lutheran World Federation and the Bishops' Commission for Ecumenical Affairs, 1967.

Lutherans and Catholics in Dialogue IV: Eucharist and Ministry. Published Jointly by Representatives of the U.S.A. Committee of the Lutheran World Federation and the Bishops' Commission for Ecumenical Affairs, 1970.

Faith and Order Findings, Montreal 1963. Augsburg Publishing House, Minneapolis, 1963.